SOCIO-CULTURAL LEADERSHIP

Socio-Cultural Leadership

The Art of Restructuring Schools Through
Research-Based Principal Leadership

Desmond K. Blackburn

iUniverse, Inc.
New York Bloomington

Socio-Cultural Leadership
The Art of Restructuring Schools Through Research-Based Principal Leadership

iUniverse books may be ordered through booksellers or by contacting:

iUniverse
1663 Liberty Drive
Bloomington, IN 47403
www.iuniverse.com
1-800-Authors (1-800-288-4677)

ISBN: 978-0-595-52826-4 (pbk)
ISBN: 978-0-595-62878-0 (ebk)

Printed in the United States of America

iUniverse rev. date: 1/21/09

For the children living in poverty and the
school leaders committed to giving them a quality education

Contents

Chapter 1

Contextual Foundation

According to Baker, Betebenner, and Linn (2002), the *No Child Left Behind Act* of 2001 required schools and school districts to carefully examine the teaching and learning process and its relationship to poor performing students. The public outcry is deafening as politicians are called upon to make the improvement of public schools a significant portion of their political agendas. While the public's outcry is deafening, it is absolutely well-deserved. Walk the halls of any school in America, and the average citizen would be shocked (maybe not) to find that we can predict, with near certainty, which students will go on and live lives of social and economic prosperity. Likewise, we can predict who will not.

We can make those predictions by simply asking some basic demographic questions of each student. Which ethnic group do you belong to? What is the primary language spoken in your home? What is the highest level of education attained by your parents? What is the approximate income earned in your home? Do you live with both biological parents? Are you a boy or a girl? It is certainly horrific, yet true, to know that the answers to such non-academic questions will, in fact, predict how well the individual student will do in school; subsequently in life.

The student demographic characteristics mentioned above that have been found to be highly correlated with academic outcomes have become so plentiful that we have had to take steps to break down such massive quantities of information into manageable pieces. Let's say, just as a silly example, that we have a 13-year-old Latino young man whose semi-illiterate parents speak very little to no English. This young man lives with ten members of his nuclear and extended family members in a two-bedroom apartment in the heart of an American inner-city. In reality, there are far too many detrimental characteristics for his school's caregivers (teachers, counselors, principals) to remember. This student is a minority. His parents do not speak the language. They themselves are uneducated. He has cramped, insufficient living conditions. He is likely without appropriate health care and/or a balanced diet.

Each characteristic, in and of itself, is enough to make the possibility of attaining a sound education doubtful. He is the unfortunate owner of a multitude of detrimental factors. These characteristics are burdensome for this young man and even more burdensome on school personnel. Therefore, for managerial purposes, he is classified with his peers who share common demographics and then simply labeled, "at-risk." Under our current educational system, this young man's chances for a pre-mature death and/or incarceration are exponentially greater than his chances of someday being the owner of a high school diploma. Am I the only person who feels it is an absolute disgrace to our country that these predictions can be made without even asking what his IQ is?

Because I am a public school educator, my philosophical position is not meant to be accusatory towards public education. The challenging, significantly paradoxical, expectations of school leaders are countless. Persons who occupy positions of leadership, within schools and school districts, are expected to manage sufficiently a host of social ills, while simultaneously being evaluated by a small number of objective measures. Likewise, school policy makers and practitioners spend an abundance of time dealing with dysfunctions of a greater society (drug abuse, gang violence, teenage pregnancy, poverty, unemployment, etc.). By "dealing with," I mean to say that the above mentioned societal dysfunctions are extremely evident in America's schools; therefore, they threaten the level of instruction that educators can provide. They also threaten the amount of learning that students can retain reasonably. Yet, Holme (2002) stated that schools will be evaluated based on their ability to enhance the scholastic achievement of poor, disadvantaged students of color.

Arguably, herein lies the most incredible piece of irony in the expectations bestowed upon educators. Educators (teachers, counselors, and principals) are trained in areas of curriculum, instruction, class scheduling, and budgeting. Yet, if there is threat of gang violence in schools, they are expected to extinguish it; if teenage pregnancy is on the rise, they are expected to reduce it; if children are using and selling illegal drugs, they are expected to smother that problem as well. As teachers, counselors, and administrators successfully engage in such activities, despite lack of formal and/or informal training in such matters, that dissuade gang membership, discourage adolescent sexual behavior, and aggressively fight the war on drugs (just to name a few), unfortunately they reduce the amount of time spent on reading, writing, and arithmetic.

Nevertheless, the public's definition of a "job well-done" hinges upon student achievement and student achievement only. The primary indicator of enhanced student achievement is positive changes on standardized tests. Decker and Decker (2003) acknowledge these demands by stating that educators have been blamed for failing test scores, increased school violence, rising dropout rates, a shortage of good teachers, and a lack of basic skills. Critical mental models held by the constituents of our federal, state, and local leaders, such as the aforementioned by Decker and Decker, validate the reasons why educational reform is at the top of many political agendas.

While the founding fathers guaranteed us a separation between church and state (believe it or not), they fell shy of protecting the noble profession of education from the impact of politics. Subsequently, principals face an abundance of political pressures and critiques. Foster (2004) refers to the current political climate with regard to public education as the *standards movement* in which all students are held accountable for learning, regardless of their backgrounds.

> The standards movement has, of course, garnered enough statistics about the so-called weaknesses of the educational system to fuel a rather large public confidence gap; although the accuracy of such statistics has been challenged, there is no doubt that they have served a political purpose in establishing a particular narrative about the failures of American schools. (Foster, p.177)

Justified or not, the politically driven demand that public schools improve, despite the well-documented, seemingly insurmountable social obstacles is bona fide. The confidence gap that Foster alludes to is a necessary evil due to the almighty dollar. School systems constantly vie for public resources against other publicly funded programs such as social security, law enforcement, transportation, parks and recreation, and so on. Since most

Americans pay taxes that are directly appropriated to schools, they are prone to believe that schools should meet their expectations. Schools and school systems will fail to meet their obligation and will continue to widen the public gap in confidence without effective principals leading the charge; which will hinder the appropriations of tax dollars to education. Without the existence of strong, site-based leadership; the type of leadership that does not view dysfunctions of society as detractors from his or her primary purpose, but as the hub of school leadership, educators cannot hope to regain the public's confidence.

Schools are becoming the places where politicians are focusing on changes that address a plethora of social ills and past inequalities. Principals are pressured, politically and otherwise, at a level that is unmatched by any other time in history to attend to the moral purpose of school and the challenges brought on by poverty, in particular. Currently, our schools are plagued by personal beliefs that suggest society is crumbling, and educators cannot meet academic demands while being faced with societal demands. These beliefs, in my opinion, must be challenged and altered.

Beliefs, I assert, dictate actions. If educators do not believe they can make a difference in the lives of children and the community at large, their actions will follow suit. Such belief systems ignore the moral purpose of school activity and especially school leadership. What is the solution? The solution is that school culture must adopt a set of commonly held beliefs that support the notion that public education is meant to serve the greater community, and that effective leadership at all levels of the system, specifically the school principal level, is the only way that public education will fulfill its obligation to society.

The mission should be to establish a means of erecting, and then multiplying exponentially, an abundance of successful schools for society. The very first step in creating a successful school is to have the audacity to define what a *successful school* is.

The conceptual framework, driven by a host of historical and contemporary popular opinions with regard to public education, used to develop *Socio-Cultural Leadership*, affirms that a successful school is a place where the leadership is shared. The people need to be change-oriented with the commonly held and communicated moral purpose of inspiring an entire local community to create a rejuvenated commitment to the teaching and learning process, especially for at-risk students who are typically children of poverty. This can only happen through effective principal leadership.

An effective principal, especially when serving a community where many of the residents are living in poverty, must lead the efforts in that community to take society's problems on with a vengeance in order to alter the natural course of things—making it so that the label at-risk does not become an automatic death/jail sentence. Checkley (2004) states:

> Being boss is about conveying to staff that there is a larger purpose to our work. Being boss means tapping into that yearning in human beings to be involved in something important and grand. Really great leaders, whether they are in education or industry, have this capacity to exude something—charisma, perhaps, and intentionally—that makes other people say, 'I will follow you.' It's not just that these people are interested in pleasing the boss; they want to bring into reality new or improved product. In education, that product is increased student achievement and changed lives. (p. 72)

The principal's role is overwhelmed by intangibles that are crucial to the effectiveness of a school's operation. Creating a commonly held, morally based vision and setting the stage for innovation and change are the standards that school leaders, in particular principals, will have to live up to. This takes on additional significance when educators address the needs of underperforming students from communities weighed down with poverty and the challenges that accompany poor students. If educators are truly committed to reaching all students in this age of accountability, then it is the principal who must provide for new and innovative ways of reaching students.

As previously stated, the conceptual framework that served as a foundation to the creation of Socio-Cultural Leadership had at its center a morally based expectation of principals to ensure student achievement gains despite the challenges of poverty. These two facets of the conceptual framework (moral purpose of school and the impact of poverty) will be addressed in the next two sections.

Moral Purpose of School

Historically, the activity of schooling in America has been seen by many as one laced with a moral overtone. Dewey (1909) supported a notion that

the moral responsibility of schooling was to society: "The school is funda-
mentally an institution erected by society to do a certain specific work—to
exercise a certain specific function in maintaining the life and advancing the
welfare of society" (p. 7). This concept of moral purpose has influenced modern ideologies with regard to the purpose of education.

Foster (2004) offers a contemporary view to Dewey on the notion of
the moral purpose of schooling. "The school organization has come to be
seen in an almost totally instrumental way: as a tool to achieve those social
goals deemed important in a particular period but almost always focusing
on the development of a productive and employable citizen" (p. 186). These
two perspectives (Dewey and Foster) offer tremendous insight for principals.
The paradoxical expectations of school leaders are, in fact, representative of
the original thoughts of the purpose of schooling in America. Society did,
rightfully so, expect schools to dissuade gang violence and drug abuse while
simultaneously ensuring pupils are able to read, write, and compute with
proficiency—therefore increasing the employability of students and the
likelihood that they would become self-sufficient, positive contributors to
society.

Fullan (2003) and Smith (2004) are two people who have provided key
directions to the idea of embracing moral purpose as the central theme in
public education in America; additional contemporary validation of Dewey's
moral purpose of education. In fact, Fullan (2003) provided ardent insight
into why the public is so involved and so demanding of public education
and its leaders. "The best case for public education has always been that it is
a common good. Everyone, ultimately has a stake in the caliber of schools,
and education is everyone's business" (p. 3). Meaning, since all persons have a
stake in the quality of schools, all persons have an inherit sense of entitlement
to how schools function.

As additional testimony that Dewey's historical framework of the
moral purpose of schooling has influenced contemporary scholarly views,
Smith (2004) offers the following: "An essential characteristic of a modern
democratic society is therefore, a citizenry that not only prepares individuals
to be responsible for their own well-being but who contribute to the well being
of the larger community" (p. 2). Once again, more direction to school leaders
to willingly take on the occupation of helping students not to make self-
destructive decisions (gangs, drugs, pre-marital sex, etc.) while arming them
with the intellectual capacity to move society forward positively by building

better roads, curing illness, taking on positions of political leadership, and growing the economy through business ownership.

While many people have roles to play in order for society's desires to be fulfilled, arguably no role is more momentous than that of a school principal. "Schools, through the principal's leadership, should encourage and provide to students: positive emotional support, a nutritious diet, an atmosphere free of undue pressure but with high academic expectations for all learners, social interaction, and choices in learning" (Nunnelley et al. 2003, p. 53). With such distinct direction from the research community, why are practitioners often so resistant in taking on the needs of the school, as determined by the community that surrounds the school? Why do teachers frown at the idea of having to be not only teachers, but mothers, fathers, clergymen, police officers, doctors, and dieticians? Why do principals also frown at the idea of not only having to manage a school, but take full responsibility for the insufficient preparation novice educators receive from college? Why do principals also resist the notion that they too must manage local political relationships with school board members, community activists, mayors, and city commissioners? My assertion as to the explanation of the resistance is tied into the lack of concrete understanding on the parts of school personnel and, perhaps more importantly, the lack of empathy of those individuals who give educators their marching orders, so to speak. Plainly put, today's educator is faced with directives that are clear, yet vague.

The contemporary ambiguity in society's wishes becomes painfully evident to all persons responsible for public education, especially principals. Are schools in the business of creating high-achieving students based on high-stakes testing? Are schools in the business of ensuring a child's social, emotional, and physical well-being? Once again, Dewey (1909), one of the founding fathers of public education, can be looked at to bring synergy to answers of both questions. His advice is as germane now as it was when he articulated these points originally, close to one hundred years ago. "The business of the educator—whether parent or teacher—is to see to it that the greatest possible number of ideas acquired by children and youth are acquired in such a vital way that they become moving ideas, motive-forces in the guidance of conduct" (p. 2). Likewise, Michael Fullan, seen by many as the modern day authority on school reform, suggests similarly, "In schools, good things are enhanced student performance, increased capacity of teachers, greater involvement of parents and community members, engagement of students, all-around satisfaction and enthusiasm about going further and greater pride for all in the system" (Fullan, 2001, p. 10). The two previously stated messages from Dewey (1909) and Fullan (2001) have the potential of coming across as paradoxical demands on the principal. As the creation of Socio-Cultural Leadership evolved, it became my intent to show how they are one in the same.

Student-Teacher Cultural Gap

As the historically based moral purpose of schooling is influenced by contemporary issues such as the growing impact of poverty, educators are forced to engage in activities that are foreign to the current status quo in order to combat the challenges of poverty. Among other ills of society, poverty has been especially difficult to manage in schools. "One of the reasons it is getting more and more difficult to conduct school as we have in the past is that the students who bring the middle class culture with them are decreasing in numbers, and the students who bring the poverty culture with them are increasing in numbers" (Payne 1998, p. 79). This is a significant reality.

Shields (2004) offers additional insight, and potential ramifications, on overcoming issues related to poverty in schools.

> It is well documented that the large majority of educators in developed countries come from what may loosely be called the middle class and, hence, may find it difficult to understand, communicate with, or develop meaningful relationships with students from working class families, children whose families receive social assistance, or those who live in other impoverished situations. The insidious part is that without even being aware of it, educators often make decisions about students' ability, programs, and suitable career paths based on class. (p. 120)

This comment from Shields warrants further examination. Plainly said, there is a huge gap between the socio-cultural backgrounds of educators and students. From the multitude of socio-cultural factors in schools, there is a very chaotic, often ignored; dynamic that impacts educators' ability to enhance student achievement. What, you ask, is the exact impact of socio-cultural factors on student achievement?

Unequivocally, for some reason, this part of my book was the most difficult to write. There was no shortage of ideas and/or concerns on my part. The difficulty was finding books, journal articles, and research studies that could adequately support my position on the impact of socio-cultural factors on student achievement and school improvement efforts.

As seen in other parts of the book, I assumed a sincere obligation to ensure that the concepts of this book were deeply rooted in theory. I did not want this book to be just another author pontificating all over the place. Unable to find relative theory that could substantiate my thoughts effectively caused a great deal of frustration in me. My state of frustration took me to a very different place, and it provided a catalyst for me to try something unusual. I decided to articulate my meaning by telling a story.

In order to understand my story, you, the reader, are going to have to practice a high level of acceptance in the paragraphs to follow. I am going to attempt to place you in a contextual setting that I feel will be an optimal position to understand the socio-cultural forces that make public school education so very challenging. So, please comply with my requests and allow yourself to be placed in my context. You are going to be required to play an active role in this journey by assuming a character in my story as well as interacting with the other characters. Trust me. There is a point here somewhere!

> ***Self Reflection.*** First, let's start with who you are. You are a veteran teacher with 20 years of classroom experience (or lack thereof). You were born and raised in a traditional middle-class family. Your mother and father were both hard-working parents and your family consisted of a biological mother, a biological father, 2.5 children, and a dog. As a child, life for you was very simple; you assumed the norms and values that your parents demonstrated for you. As a matter of fact, they did such a good job raising you that you are now the mother or father in a family quite similar to the one in which you grew up. Likewise, your 2.5 kids succumb to your will, and walk in your way. Life is grand. Life is grand until the first day of a new school year, and you sit at your desk as your students walk into your classroom for the very first time. Before I go any further, please reflect on who you are and what you bring into that classroom in terms of socio-cultural values and expectations. As your students come walking in, you develop an interest in two students in particular. I'll call them Alex and Sidney. All you know

about these students right now is what you can see by way of their appearance.

Meet Alex. At this point, I am going to do my best at giving you a head-to-toe description of Alex. Starting with the head, Alex's hair is in braids that you can hardly see because of a blue bandana being worn. Alex is wearing a t-shirt that seems to be five sizes too large with a huge picture of a recently murdered rap star on the front of it. Alex's neck has a gold chain around it with a pendant at the end of it that looks like a semi-automatic handgun. On Alex's left forearm, you notice a tattoo that reads, "Thug 4-Life." Moving on to Alex's lower body, you notice that Alex is wearing blue jeans that seem 10 sizes too big. On the upper-right portion of these jeans you see a spray-painted picture of a slain civil rights leader. For some reason that you cannot imagine, Alex's left pant leg is rolled up just above the knee. Alex is wearing what seems to be an expensive pair of Reebok tennis shoes. However, you do not understand what makes them so expensive because they do not even have the standard Reebok emblem on them. Instead Alex's shoes have the number 50 inscribed on the side. Alex does not say much except to tell you that Alex is not the name this student prefers. Alex informs you that the name you are to use when communicating is "A-Dawg." When Alex says this your eyes are drawn back to the facial area where you notice that Alex has strategically placed three gold caps over three different teeth. At this point your eyes have fixated themselves on Alex. That is, until Sidney walks in giving you a reason to look at something else.

Meet Sidney. Let me describe the next 30 seconds of your life as you observe Sidney's appearance from head-to-toe. Starting with the head, you notice that Sidney's hair consists of a long black pony-tale. Sidney is wearing a chain, but not around the neck. Instead this chain connects the earring to the nose ring to the piece of metal that is sticking out of Sidney's chin. You notice mascara on Sidney's left eye, but none on the right eye. You also notice blush on Sidney's right cheek, but none on the left cheek. Sidney is wearing a black t-shirt that seems to be one or two sizes too small. You really cannot make out the picture on the front of the t-shirt. For some reason, the picture looks like a bloody, gory crime seen. Under the picture are the words, "Rest in Peace." On Sidney's left forearm you see a tattoo of a tombstone that reads, "Sidney–01/13/2001." You look down at your watch to notice today's date, August 25, 2007. Sidney's pants are all black and they too seem a couple of sizes too small and they only go down to the mid-calf area. These are cargo-style pants with bulging pockets. Sidney is wearing black stockings. In fact the only splash of color on this ensemble comes by way of the high-top, hot-pink Converse All-Star tennis shoes that Sidney is wearing. Because these are the same type of shoes you wore as a child, you begin to connect with Sidney. That is until Sidney opens the mouth in order to quietly utter the following words, "Don't call me Sidney. I only answer to Marylyn." This is when you notice that there is a huge chunk of shiny metal protruding from Sidney's tongue.

Your Thoughts? At this point, what preconceived ideas do you have of these two students? I know we are only two minutes into the first time that you are meeting these two students, but you have made some judgments simply based on your observations of them. If you have not, may I suggest that you do not really know yourself, or you are lying! These ideas that you have of these students are going to impact your interaction with them. Do you know how? Do you know when? Before going on, I am going to ask you to go back and read the descriptions of Alex and Sidney again. After reading the descriptions again, what do you notice? Have I left anything out? Do you have any idea of the race, gender, or social class of Alex and Sidney? This is a trick question because I know you think, based on their descriptions, that you know their race, gender, and social class. Hold on tight to your bookmark because I am going to give you some additional information on Alex and Sidney.

More on Alex. First of all Alex is short for Alexandria Goldman. She is a 15-year-old Caucasian female with one 8-year-old sibling. Alex lives in a middle-class neighborhood with her biological father, who owns a small accounting firm, and her biological stay-at-home mother. Both of her parents have tried desperately to get her to conform to their socio-cultural values that are entrenched in their strong Jewish faith.

More on Sidney. Sidney is not short for anything. He is a 15-year-old African American male with four older siblings whom he rarely sees because he lives with his maternal grandmother and an aunt in a small lower-income community on the edge of a large urban city. His siblings live with his paternal grandmother. Regardless of his grandmother's attempts, he absolutely refuses to attend church with his grandmother. She was born and raised in the Pentecostal church.

Reactions. Let's be honest, when these students first walked in you categorized these students as "abnormal," right? As you learned more about their race, gender, and social class, you are thinking that they are not even "normally" abnormal. It seems like a lot doesn't it? Let me remind you that you are only five minutes into a student-teacher relationship that is scheduled to last for 180 days. What are you thinking? Are you thinking? Are you thinking about how your preconceived ideas regarding their appearance were going to impact your interactions with them? Have you acknowledged that you actually have these preconceived ideas? Have you realized that these students are totally disconnected from their families, their peers, their communities? Are you thinking about ways to connect to these students? Are you wondering how you are going to manage the socio-cultural chaos that exists in your classroom? Or, did you just take attendance and jump right in to your attempt of forcing the state-mandated curriculum down their throats? If Alex or Sidney gets fed up with you as you review rigorous and relevant curriculum and stands up in the middle of your presentation of the lesson plans you created five years ago and shouts out, "This is bull-shit," do you have him or her immediately removed from class and charged with defiance?

Disclaimer. The scenario that I described is being played out everyday in every public school in America. I apologize for not offering any solutions. Right now, all I have are questions? I'll end with the question with which I began this little scenario—What is the impact of socio-cultural factors on student achievement and school improvement?

The story above is merely an example of the complexities seen in schools around race, class, gender, and religion, just to name a few. There are far too many to give adequate attention to. In my development of Socio-Cultural Leadership, I sought to deal with social class primarily and focus on poverty's impact in schools. In my travels as an educator and a researcher, I found poverty to be the most challenging factor in moving student achievement forward.

Politics in Education

In addition to school leaders finding it difficult to manage the impact of poverty on student achievement, community leaders and community leadership, while the potential is there for them to be supporters of principals, are often seen as hindrances. They (local, state, and federal political leaders) often apply unwavering pressure on school systems to conquer larger societal ills that they, themselves, have proven to be inadequate in changing. Schools are simply microcosms of the communities that surround them. As I have said to people before, it is difficult for schools to improve when societal downfalls that contribute to a less-than-adequate education have not been pursued with due diligence by our elected officials.

I find it desperately difficult not to be critical of political leadership. In society, we have the "haves" and we have the "have-nots." My indictment is that we, society at large, do not have enough "haves" that truly want to see the "have-nots" share in the American Dream. The "haves" I am referring to are those of us who are citizens of this country who possess resources (intellectual, financial, political, etc.), which if shared, could increase the likelihood that people currently living in poverty could someday meet with some level of prosperity.

As sociologists have studied the inner-city, they have found that many of the social problems found there are less the result of cultural values and more the result of low levels of public investment in infrastructure, poor public housing, inadequate health care, poor schools, and a disappearing employment base (Wilson 1996, as cited in Bulman 2002, p. 258). Ginwright (2000) noted similar findings.

> Unlike their suburban counterparts, urban schools are forced to grapple with the day-to-day reality of poverty, joblessness, and the consequent crime that has become common for poor communities. For many urban schools, the needs of their students far outweigh the meager resources available to them. The lack of basic school supplies and materials, deteriorating facilities, lack of parent involvement, and unprepared students all create greater challenges for schools in poor urban communities. (p. 89)

I am unequivocally supportive of the moral responsibility of public education in that we are to meet the needs of society. Politicians, in addition to writing the next piece of unfunded legislation, need to support education, conceptually, financially, and most importantly, socially.

Nevertheless, the literature is supportive of the fact that schools, and people that occupy them, can and should make a positive difference in the lives of children living in poverty. As an educator, I could go on and on about what needs to be done for us. Instead, I prefer, from an educational systemic point of view, to look in the mirror for answers. I am undeniably sold on the notion that while educators do not control all of the variables that contribute to improved student achievement; we do control enough of them. For guidance, I once again return to Fullan (2003) for our moral responsibility as educators.

> Moral purpose of the highest order is having a system where all students learn, the gap between high and low performance becomes greatly reduced, and what people learn enables them to be successful citizens and workers in a morally based knowledge society. (Fullan 2003, p. 29)

One, all students are not learning at acceptable rates. Two, there continues to be too large of a gap between high and low performance; this gap is often moderated by demographic characteristics of students (race, class, gender, etc.). If educators deeply believed that they are in place to serve needs, just the mental shift alone would get them going on the right track.

Dewey (1909) and Foster (2004) both agree that schools have an unambiguous, morally-based obligation to society.

> Interest in community welfare, an interest that is intellectual and practical, as well as emotional—an interest, that is to say, in perceiving whatever makes for social order and progress, and in carrying these principles into execution—is the moral habit to which all the special school habits must be related if they are to be animated by the breath of life. (Dewey 1909, p. 17)

The *No Child Left Behind Act* of 2001 represents a host of bipartisan, politically driven, societal demands of public school educators. Specifically, society is demanding that all children be able to meet stated proficiencies tested through high stakes assessments. The responsibility of effective schooling is placed squarely on the shoulders of school-based leaders, the principals. The most poignant challenges that principals face as they try to meet societal expectations come from the impact of poverty. The existence of poverty in schools has a negative, direct impact on standardized student achievement measures.

While I support the argument that poverty is the most important social consideration to attend to in moving student achievement forward, educational researchers, practitioners, and policy makers are not collectively sure that poverty is the primary factor to consider when we focus on school improvement efforts. In fact, there are some segments of the scholarly community that support race over poverty as the primary factor to consider.

Race versus Poverty

There are a number of indicators to suggest that race warrants the majority of the attention as we try to target a factor that is consistently shown to have a direct relationship with poor student achievement. All across America, children of color are scoring the lowest on standardized tests as compared to Caucasian and Asian children (Johnson 2003). Additionally when we speak of children of color, while many non-Caucasian ethnicities exist, we are often referring to one segment of the non-Caucasian community—African Americans.

Within the historical context of public education in America, African American students have been seen as the group most affected by the ineffectiveness of public education. Today's data are as reflective of these disparities as any other time in history, especially for African American males. When compiling educational statistics in most schools, school districts, or sates, African American males are much more likely to have the lowest grade point averages. They are most likely to be retained in a grade. They are most likely to be removed form class/school for disobedience. They are most likely to be labeled as emotionally handicapped and/or learning disabled. The coincidental nature of these educational facts is not without accusatory doubts. According to Tyack (1974), "To have been born black was normally to have been labeled a failure—an inferiority all too often justified by a bogus science—as millions of Negro children learned in school systems which were consciously or unwittingly racist" (p. 217).

Recently compiled statistical data suggest that race, particularly the African American race, is a more reliable factor to hold constant when looking at school reform efforts meant to target underperforming students. This has proven to be a costly mistake. These reform efforts focus solely on overcoming "blackness" in order to achieve in school. This is to suggest that being black is the equivalent to a social disorder. This is a huge mistake in thinking.

As a society, we are missing the boat in a big way. If one looks deeper, you would find that African American students fall behind in school because they are more likely to have been born out of wedlock to a single mother who did not receive adequate health care; least likely to be enrolled in a rigorous pre-school program; least likely to have a computer in the home; least likely to have a parent or guardian participate in school activities; least likely to receive adequate healthcare; least likely to be exposed to the arts; least likely to travel out of state or country for additional cultural enhancement; least likely to own the home they live in.

Hence, African Americans are more likely to be living in poverty and; therefore, are suffering from aspects that derive from their socio-cultural condition; not their blackness. According to Dalaker (2001), after nearly a decade of economic growth, just over 11 percent of the American population remained poor at the turn of the twenty-first century, including over a fifth of African Americans (Iceland 2003, p. 499). This observation suggests that there are disproportionate numbers of African American people who are living in poverty. These numbers are staggering. This means that African Americans, as of 2001, made up 11 percent of the population but 20 percent of the people living in poverty; nearly twice as many.

Using a case study approach to evaluate the transformational efforts at an urban high school in Oakland, California, Ginwright (2000) was able to refute the notion that racial considerations, instead of the impact of poverty, should play a larger role in school reform considerations. He offers the following explanation to this widespread myth:

> Because urban communities largely comprise ethnic minorities (Asian Americans, Mexican Americans, African Americans), multicultural reform efforts are largely constructed around racial identities and ignore the complex ways in which identity is constructed through the influence and interaction of other variables such as social class, gender, age, and physical ability. (p. 88)

His explanation acknowledges the relationship between poverty and ethnicity, as well as the similarities of the impact of both on the educational process. Nevertheless, his findings support the idea that poverty has the highest impact on schools. School leaders need to focus on combating the effects of poverty in order to close, and eventually eliminate, the achievement gap.

> If we continue to be sold racial identity as the panacea to ethnic poor and working-class schools and communities we will also pay the price of simplifying the complexity of oppression and injustice to mere racial categories. If we pay this price, we will misdiagnose the reasons why millions of poor children come to school hungry, why thousands of young black boys engage in deadly gang violence, and simply why America's schools have been unable to address these problems. (Ginwright 2000, p. 102)

Conceptually speaking, Socio-Cultural Leadership is supportive of the argument that poverty should play a bigger role in school reform efforts than ethnicity. Furthermore, Socio-Cultural Leadership sought to identify specific instructional leadership activities that are evident in the day-to-day actions of principals that serve communities of high poverty. The focus is on instruction because enhanced pedagogy is the only way that public schools will effectively combat the burdening impact that poverty has on student achievement. "It is the research on learning that must be addressed if we are to work successfully with students from poverty" (Payne 1998, p. 119).

Finding high-yield instructional leadership activities that were conducive to better student achievement, in low income communities in particular, was a difficult undertaking. We, the education community, have not solidified our definition of teaching and learning. We also have not determined how we measure the effectiveness of such efforts.

Teaching and Learning Explored

"Nationally and internationally, a renewed focus on learning and teaching has brought a change in role and focus for principals from site managers to instructional leaders" (Yep and Chrispeels, 2004, p. 3). What is learning? What is teaching? What is the responsibility of a principal when it comes to building a school culture with "teaching and learning" as the nucleus, especially with regard to students that come from communities of poverty?

The *No Child Left Behind Act* of 2001 requires that states develop and implement high and rigorous standards for academic attainment, and then monitor students' progress toward these standards with annual tests in reading and mathematics in grades three through ten. If test scores go up, did teaching improve? Did learning occur? This is a debate that has dominated many conversations among educational scholars, practitioners, and lay persons.

The conceptual foundation of Socio-Cultural Leadership will not seek to prove or disprove the notion that increased student achievement is evidenced by increasing scores on high stakes tests. Instead, Socio-Cultural Leadership recognizes that society has spoken; and subsequently seeks to fulfill the demands of society as defined by a synthesized interpretation of existing literature and policies which affirm that an increase in test scores and the reduction of the achievement gap are two primary indicators of a school being effective.

In 1909, Dewey articulated points that can and should be considered by today's principals in order for them to stay focused on the "real" work. "He is to be a worker, engaged in some occupation that will be of use to society, and which will maintain his own independence and self-respect" (p. 9). Dewey's point, and others like it, may be misconstrued to advise principals to mitigate the critical analysis of student achievement data as one way to measure the effectiveness of their instructional leadership abilities.

On the contrary, the critical analysis of school data, along with data-based decision making, is an important piece in building effective schools. School leaders, especially principals, must caution themselves not to dismiss data findings as irrelevant and/or coincidental. By the same token, school leaders have to be cognizant of oversimplifying the data and believing that they know exactly what caused the data results.

During times of increasing focus on accountability and content standards, it is more important than ever to remember the role schools play in the development of students' lives. When school leaders use the absence of learning gains on accountability measures to publicly endorse a "teach to the test" philosophy in their schools where the curriculum is overwhelmed by drill and kill practice of basic skills and children are not allowed to explore their social context using critical thinking abilities, the resulting school culture is one that does not get students, especially students living in poverty, any closer to being able to lead productive lives in a democratic society. Although students' test scores are improving as teachers gear their instruction around the test, it has been proven that student achievement gains are higher, sustainable, and applicable when children are exposed to learner-centered instructional strategies that encourage students, especially economically disadvantaged students, to think critically; to read, write, and compute around critical content.

Throughout this book, you will note that I take the position of advocate on a variety of matters. This is one: Socio-Cultural Leadership WILL NOT endorse "teach to the test" practices. The test is the test; it should guide curriculum and instruction, but it should not dictate it. We need not become slaves to the test. Rather, we should focus on building better students. By better, I mean students who not only regurgitate facts, but can incorporate critical thinking around those facts to create new knowledge.

Again, the intent is not to negate the significance of a student's ability to perform at acceptable rates within critical content areas as measured by standardized tests. Reading ability is central to students' learning, to their success in school, and ultimately to their success in life. The intent of Socio-Cultural Leadership is to show how learning can and should be defined more by our relationships and engagement strategies, with impoverished children especially.

Underprivileged students often embrace how they are taught as opposed to what they are taught (Payne 1998). Students reported more positive forms of motivation and greater academic engagement when they perceived their teachers were using learner-centered practices that involve caring, establishing higher order thinking, honoring student voices, and adapting instruction to individual needs (Meece 2003).

There are conditions that are specific to children of poverty that impact what they need to learn and the type of culture that is most conducive to learning it. As the leader of a high-poverty school, the principal must ensure that the conditions for this culture exist. Therefore, the principal must be an effective instructional leader in terms of being the primary catalyst in transforming school culture to improve student achievement, especially among underperforming student populations and to use high-yield instructional strategies to accomplish this.

Socio-Cultural Leadership's Position on Management

Many decisions that principals are required to make in schools are business oriented such as procurement, facilities management and supplier contracts. In addition, "Conflict, pressure, and time are factors which clearly impinge upon the work of schools" (Heany 2001, p. 202) and subsequently need to be managed. As a matter of fact, in 1996 the Interstate School Leaders Licensure Consortium (ISLLC) stated as one out of its six standards, the need for school leaders to exercise managerial competence. "A school administrator is an educational leader who promotes the success of all students by ensuring management of the organization, operations, and resources for a safe, efficient, and effective learning environment" (ISLLC 1996, p. 14). These "transactional" activities, while significant to school operations, have been conspicuously absent from results of studies that have measured leadership traits of school leaders that have been successful in school improvement endeavors.

In fact, Clark, Petzko, and Valentine (2004) reported their findings from a study sponsored by the National Association of Secondary School Principals (NASSP) of the leadership traits of ninety-eight highly successful principals in the United States. Not only were the principals surveyed, but their responses were compared to the responses of students and parents as well. Among other more notable findings, the study found that these highly successful principals were excellent resource managers, but they were considered as such because of other characteristics of their leadership styles. "They used a combination of social leadership, communication skills, vision, commitment, and the ability to empower and engage others to garner resources and then distribute them in accordance with the school vision" (p. 105). This implies that their perceived excellence in the area of transactional activities was a byproduct of their more transformational style of leadership.

The leaders were instrumental in establishing a school culture of collaboration and morality. They created work environments where relationships were trusting and respectful. The principals used formal and informal change processes to establish professional learning communities that supported their commitment to success for each student. They created ways to personalize the educational experiences for their students. (p. 114)

It is in this vein that Socio-Cultural Leadership was generated. And, it is in this vein that Socio-Cultural Leadership deemphasizes technical managerial prowess, on the part of the principal, as the panacea to increased student achievement indicators.

Not all children are reading, writing, or computing at acceptable rates. The gap between high and low performance continues to widen. These two facts are exacerbated when poverty is introduced. Honing a principal's managerial skills around such transactional activities as budgeting and time management will not yield, has not yielded the type of changes needed in order to improve the dilapidated educational product now seen in many schools, especially in those schools that serve large numbers of students living in poverty.

While organizational leadership theorists and practitioners focused on transactional activities prior to the early 1990s, Bass and Avolio (1994) initiated the argument that transformational leadership was worthy of increased attention. "Transformational leadership refers to the process whereby an individual engages with others and creates a connection that raises a level of motivation and morality in both the leader and the follower" (Northouse 2001, p. 132). Murphy (2002), an authority in contemporary school leadership reform, offered very progressive thinking to the educational leadership profession by suggesting that school leaders focus their attention on three central roles: moral steward, educator, and community builder. When speaking toward the transformational expectations of school leaders, he said "It is grounded more on modeling and clarifying values and beliefs than on telling people what to do" (p. 188).

The germination of Socio-Cultural Leadership grew out of modern contextual factors that hold school leaders accountable to rising student performance standards in communities of high poverty and the complexities involved in securing, and equitably distributing, limited resources. That being said,

> The idea of the school leader as a 'monarchic,' 'autocratic' or 'paternal' executive of school has increasingly been seen as inappropriate, but viewing a school leader as a mere 'manager' or 'administrative executive' is inadequate as well, despite the managerial pressures of the present situation. (Huber 2004, p. 672)

From a practitioner's perspective, the accountability era has brought with it extreme appreciation for the standardization for resource management, leaving many school leaders without the ability to independently make managerial decisions such as school spending, personnel hiring, textbook purchases, class size, etc. This fact further deemphasizes, without eliminating, the need for heighten managerial astuteness on the part of the principal.

This is not an author's ploy to immunize school leaders totally from managerial/transactional responsibilities. Instead, Socio-Cultural Leadership is an application of Maxwell's (2004) 80/20 rule which, paraphrased, is an understanding that 80 percent of a leader's success will be attributed to 20 percent of said leader's actions. The 20 percent of a principal's actions that will lead to increased achievement for all students and a reduction in the achievement gap is the segment outlined by Socio-Cultural Leadership.

By now, you may have an understanding of the conceptual underpinnings that *Socio-Cultural Leadership* rests upon. The next section will capture completely the primary tenets of this model for school leadership. Socio-Cultural Leadership is a researched-based model for school leadership. All research will be provided to the reader.

Primary Tenets of Socio-Cultural Leadership

The demands of public education are plentiful. The challenges faced by public schools are enormous, especially for communities with high rates of poverty. While many factors influence the success rate of schools, none are more influential than the impact of effective local school leadership by way of a principal.

The existing literature suggests many aspects that impact effective school leadership, however none are more substantial than: (a) as the instructional leader, the principal must supervise and evaluate instruction to make sure that students are given optimal learning opportunities; (b) as the emotional leader, the principal must ensure that teachers are intellectually equipped, emotionally stimulated, and encouraged to assume decision-making positions of leadership in schools to increase student achievement; (c) as the community leader, the principal must inspire and/or provide incentives for communal learning that is student-centered; and (d) as the facilitator of culture, the principal must also realize the limitations of leadership on student achievement and begin to shape and reshape school culture.

To my satisfaction (admittedly), the existing literature does not suggest a form of leadership that is, in any respect, a comprehensive model of instructional leadership, community leadership, and emotional leadership with the stated purpose of transforming school culture to serve the needs of our society at large. Realizing the void in literature that existed, the importance of school leadership practices, their impact on school culture, which subsequently impacts student achievement measured by a barrage of indicators, especially in schools of high poverty, prompted my development of Socio-Cultural Leadership.

The following chapters will provide insight into the current literature and research upon which are built the four primary tenets of Socio-Cultural Leadership.

Chapter 2

The Principal as the Instructional Leader

Traditionally, instructional leadership has only been seen as one, sometimes non-essential, facet of school leadership. During the 1960s, Sullivan and Glanz (2000) found that principals exerted leadership in five primary ways: (a) developing mutually acceptable goals, (b) extending cooperative and democratic methods of supervision, (c) improving classroom instruction, (d) promoting research into educational problems, and (e) promoting educational leadership. This somewhat historical perspective called for instructional leadership to serve as merely one-fifth of a principal's primary duties. For the contemporary principal, the most universally accepted fundamental function is serving as the instructional leader of a school.

As defined by Schon (1988), instructional leadership is a process that emphasizes collegial classroom observations and focuses on support, guidance, and encouragement of reflective teaching. According to Murphy and Shipman (1999) (as cited in Giesen and Newton 2004), recent changes in society, the economy, and the political arena call for administrators to focus on issues related to educational or instructional leadership.

The research on instructional leadership also supports the fact that these principal expectations are made challenging by implications of the greater society. In other words, principals are often called on to bring resolve to matters and situations that have absolutely no impact on teaching and learning. To the educational layperson reading this book, I leave you with inadequate information to substantiate my previous statement. To the practitioner, I hope that you can vouch for the fact that I could have written another entire book just on the matters that principals must contend with that take their precious time away from the educational process.

The research is clear in stating that societal considerations are not to serve as reasons and/or excuses to the perpetuation of achievement gaps. We cannot accept that student achievement gains will be moderated by race, gender, and/or social class. If this is the natural course, then it becomes the principal's duty to alter the natural course of things.

> While post industrial societies undergo rapid cultural and technological changes that influence us both in what we learn and in how we learn, there are continuing needs to grasp basic arithmetic and linguistic ideas.... The leadership task, however, is to make these connections transparent and tangible to all. (Bogotch 2002, p. 141)

Professional Dialogue versus Staff Development

Consistent with leadership ideologies from other industries, it is paramount that principals find ways to improve the collective performance of their workforce, teachers. While there are many, many people who are hired in a school or a school district who are important in moving student achievement forward, teachers are undeniably the most essential members of the workforce. In order to increase student achievement, instructional leaders must find ways of improving instruction. In my travels, principals and other school district leaders are often misguided in their efforts. To assist in this regard, Whitaker (1997) found four essentials to share with principals.

> The principal must communicate to the staff essential beliefs that (1) all children can learn and experience success; (2) success builds upon success; (3) schools can enhance student success; and (4) learner outcomes must be clearly defined to guide instructional programs and decisions. (p. 155)

To ensure that these essential beliefs transcend themselves into achievement gains, the principal must use student assessment results to shape organizational conversation around instructional practices. "If assessment is to be meaningful and guide instruction then teachers and administrators must take the time to meet and talk about student work" (Cobb 2004, p. 387). The dialogue that Cobb (2004) is referring to, if done correctly, can take the place of, and be more productive than, popular forms of staff development.

Most "staff development" seminars and workshops that I have been a part of make use of the antiquated model of having teachers/principals play the role of disengaged students while some trainer/facilitator presents outdated, irrelevant material to them in a setting where participation is contrived at best. There is a much better way to think of staff development for the Socio-Cultural Leader. "After years of exposure to staff development 'packages' created by consultants and curriculum developers, it is now evident that when teachers concentrate on their own teaching practices they are more likely to obtain gains in student achievement" (Harris 2000, p. 6).

This should be considered a crucial point to Socio-Cultural Leadership. Gone are the days where teachers' precious, limited time should be spent being lectured to by a person who would probably be less than adequate, to say the least, in successfully managing classroom challenges that teachers must compete with in areas of high poverty. Instead, collegial, self-directed, teams of teachers who collaborate authentically with each other around matters of instruction, ignited by student achievement indicators, will prove absolutely to be a more rewarding experience. These conversations will also produce a higher level of classroom instruction.

There is not enough that can be said about the benefits of teacher collaboration. Using an action research paradigm among principals and teachers in Hong Kong, Lam, Yim, and Lam (2002) found teachers generally accepted peer coaching and found it helpful to their professional development. While these teacher-to-teacher conversations have been proven to be valuable in improving instruction and subsequently student achievement, principals should facilitate a school culture where these types of conversation are initiated by teachers; not mandated by principals.

> To change the culture of isolation, the challenge for Western educators is to keep their collaboration free from the contrived collegiality, an imposition which is not conducive to their genuine joint work on reflection about the purpose, value, and consequences of what they teach. (p. 183)

Living up to the advice given by Lam, Yim, and Lam (2002) can be a difficult test. It requires trust and patience on the part of the principal. A progressive thinking principal who has done his or her homework on the topic of teacher-to-teacher coaching will have a deep understanding of how the conversations are supposed to take shape. Pair this with a feeling that conversations are not meeting this standard and being placed under enormous pressure to increase student achievement, and the average principal may cave in and begin to drive the types of conversations that happen. It is crucial that a principal not fall into this trap. Principals must trust that well-trained, caring teachers will eventually "get there" if given enough time, autonomy, and most importantly, support.

Research on Instructional Leadership

The National Association of Elementary School Principals (NAESP 2001) identified the following standards to influence the instructional leadership behaviors of principals at both the elementary level and the secondary level:

- Lead schools in a way that puts student and adult learning at the center.
- Promote the academic success of all students by setting high expectations and high standards and organizing the school environment around school achievement.
- Create and demand rigorous content and instruction that ensures student progress toward agreed upon academic standards.
- Create a climate of continuous learning for adults that is tied to student learning.
- Use multiple sources of data as a diagnostic tool to assess, identify, and apply instructional improvement.
- Actively engage the community to create shared responsibility for student and school success.

Similarly, the National Association of Secondary School Principals (NASSP 2001) established the following criteria for principals wanting to engage in high yield instructional leadership activities:

- Implement strategies for improving teaching and learning, including putting programs and improvement efforts into action.
- Develop a vision and establish clear goals.
- Provide direction in achieving stated goals.
- Encourage others to contribute to goal achievement.

- Secure commitment to a course of action from individuals and groups.

Using data gathered from a survey of over 500 principals in the state of Illinois, McEwan (1998) found seven recommendations for principals seeking to become effective instructional leaders:

- Establish and implement instructional goals.
- Be there for your staff.
- Create a school culture and climate conducive to learning.
- Communicate the vision and mission of your school.
- Set high expectations for your staff.
- Develop teacher leaders.
- Maintain positive attitudes toward students, staff, and parents.

The following descriptors of instructional leadership were identified by the National Institute on Educational Governance, Finance, Policymaking and Management (1999):

- Instructional leaders devote time, energy, and talents to improving the quality of teaching and learning.
- Instructional leaders possess a deep understanding of teaching and learning, including new teaching methods and emphasize problem solving and student construction of knowledge.
- Instructional leaders have a strong commitment to success for all students.
- Instructional leaders are committed to improving instruction for groups of students who are not currently learning.
- Instructional leaders know how to evaluate instruction and provide feedback to teachers.
- Instructional leaders engage the whole school in continuous dialogue about what good teaching looks like.
- Instructional leaders have a presence in every classroom.
- Instructional leaders provide teachers with informed feedback, guidance, support, and professional development.

Glickman (1985) defined the following as primary principal behaviors in order to fulfill their duty as an instructional leader:

- Provide direct assistance to teachers.
- Group development.

- Staff development.
- Curriculum development.
- Action research.

The principal must lead the charge in, and use alternative approaches towards, effective staff development. As emphasized in Socio-Cultural Leadership, structured professional dialogue is an example of an alternative approach that principals can use. "Responsibility for leading the discussion may reside with the principal, a teacher recognized as proficient in the topic, or members of the group on a rotating basis" (Dufour 1991, p. 81). As I have maintained, the heedful principal can and may have to be the one to initiate these conversations; true academic growth, however, will not happen in a sustainable way until teachers are groomed and empowered to take over this task. Pajak's (1993) definition of instructional leadership affirms the emergence of dialogue which emphasizes classroom teaching, curriculum, staff development, and assisting teachers construct professional knowledge and skills.

Local, State, and Federal Reform

In the age of increased accountability and social attention on education, principals also have to be cognizant of the impact of school reform directives initiated by government at all levels. Often, teachers, especially teachers in large urban schools and school districts, are about one governmental, top-down mandate away from a loud piercing cry followed by a premature exit from the education profession. This is not an over exaggeration. In my conversations with teachers, especially teachers that are truly quality educators, their aversion towards teaching in the inner-city has less to do with the disproportionate number of needy children and more to do with the level of micromanaging scripting that often occurs at the hands of school-based and district-based leaders.

The effects of micromanaging on educators is no different than the effects noticed in every other industry or setting. Teachers who have been deprived of their professional creativity are left without an emotional/intellectual connection to their craft. This is truly unfortunate. Not only that, while micromanaging school reform efforts may, or may not, return short-term increases in standardized test scores, such efforts have not proven to be successful, if one defines success as the ability to sustain achievement of students and commitment of teachers for longer periods of time.

Across the country, I have seen school districts employ methods such as providing "combat pay" to teachers who are willing to work in hard-to-staff (inner-city) schools. In my humble opinion (maybe not so humble) these dollars could be redistributed in more productive ways. The change that is needed is not a financial one; it is a conceptual one. We must trust inner-city teachers to "do the right thing" for children just like their counterparts in affluent communities who, on average, are given higher levels of autonomy and decision-making ability on instruction, curriculum, and school-wide logistics. This is a troubling revelation. Not only do we have the "brain-drain" of higher-performing students leaving urban schools in favor of schools in suburbia; we have become absolutely systemically ineffective at hiring and retaining quality teachers in inner-city schools.

Plainly stated, we have created a separate and unequal divide in many school districts. Because students in more affluent communities come to school in a more "learner-ready" condition, we have granted teachers in those schools the opportunity to be much more autonomous in deciding what to teach and how to teach it. However, teachers working in our most fragile schools (lower socio-economic) have been all but stripped of any decision-making power regarding curriculum and/or instruction. In my humble opinion (again, maybe not so humble), herein lies the number one reason why we are unable to attract teachers to inner-city schools.

Using interview data from forty-eight teachers and fifteen administrators in five secondary schools, Leithwood, Steinbach, and Jantzi (2002) found that school leadership may serve as antidotes to negative teacher motivations when such motivations are caused by shortsighted and abrasive government implementation strategies. If such governmental reform lessens teacher-efficacy, the principal must create specific ways to motivate and inspire teachers (Whitaker, Whitaker, & Lumpa, 2000). "Through their leadership, principals should provide a belief in people, job and role diversity, high expectations, positive reinforcement, and celebrations of good performance" (p. 188).

Culturally Relevant Curriculum and Instruction

The principal, especially in economically disadvantaged areas, must facilitate a process where the curriculum is meant to enable the student to better address the dynamics of their environment. "We need to know the social situations in which the individual will have to use ability to observe, recollect, imagine, and reason, in order to have any way of telling what a training of mental powers actually means" (Dewey, 1909, p. 13). For example, students living in poverty often use grammatically incorrect language. I simply cannot resist taking a moment of personal privilege to mention the fact that children living in poverty are also disproportionately attending schools where teachers and principals do not always practice the use of appropriate English. This must stop. Teachers and principals, in high-poverty schools especially, must speak to, and around, children in grammatically correct ways.

It is often cited as well that children from poor communities are not always encouraged to engage in critical thinking activities. When children from these environments do engage in critical thinking activities it is often, because of the culture gap that exists between teacher and student, misconstrued as some type of inappropriate behavior.

> In many schools, children aren't being taught to be critical thinkers, so they aren't able to challenge the conditions they face. Critical thinking ensures that our children will be better prepared for a higher level of learning. However, when students of color display critical thinking, they are looked at as being disrespectful. When our children challenge a teacher in the classroom about educational issues, they often are sent to the Dean's office for disrupting the class. (Johnson, 2002, p. 1)

Johnson's (2002) remarks allude to a pedagogical consideration that is crucial when teaching in a high-poverty and/or high-minority environment; classroom management. Far too many school efforts are spent in an attempt to "control" students, especially in large urban schools. I have worked in economically disadvantaged communities and I have worked in more affluent communities. Based on what I have witnessed, one thing that all children have in common is that when they are intellectually challenged and socially engaged in a supportive school environment, acts of defiance, disruption, etc, are drastically lower. Again, I have found this to be true when social class is held constant and/or varied.

While doing extensive research and consulting in high-poverty schools, Noguera (2003) cited the following: "In most cases, what separates those who experience frequent behavior problems and those who do not is their ability to keep their students focused on learning and intellectually engaged" (p. 347). He and other authors recognize the need for cultural transformation in schools and provide principals with specific direction in this regard.

First, we must recognize that we are all cultural beings, with our own beliefs, biases, and assumptions about human behavior.... Second, we must acknowledge the cultural, racial, ethnic, and class differences that exist among people.... Finally, culturally responsive classroom management requires that teachers are mindful not to reflect and perpetuate discriminatory practices of the larger society. (Weinstein, Curran, & Tomlinson-Clarke, 2003, p. 270)

Weinstein, Curran, and Tomlinson-Clarke (2003) explored this area of instructional leadership further to recommend the following tasks that should be required from teachers teaching in high-poverty schools:

These tasks include (a) creating a physical setting that supports academic and social goals, (b) establishing expectations for behavior, (c) communicating with students in culturally consistent ways, (d) developing a caring classroom environment, (e) working with families, and (f) using appropriate interventions to assist students with behavior problems. (p. 270)

They suggest these tasks in order to create school environments that embrace instructional strategies that are culturally responsive. "Culturally responsive classroom managers understand that the ultimate goal of classroom management is not to achieve compliance or control, but to provide all students with equitable opportunities for learning" (p. 275).

Adding to the literature on behavior management, especially in high-poverty schools, Shukla-Mehta and Albin (2003) suggest the following strategies to prevent behavioral escalation:

- Reinforce calm and on-task behaviors
- Know the triggers
- Pay attention to anything unusual about the student's behavior
- Do not escalate along with the student
- Offer students opportunities to display responsible behavior
- Intervene early in the sequence
- Understand how such behavioral incidents ended in the past
- Know the function of problem behaviors
- Use good judgment about which behaviors to punish
- Use extinction procedures wisely

- Teach students socially appropriate behavior to replace problem behavior
- Teach academic survival skills and set students up for success. (p. 51)

The literature on instructional leadership, especially in high-poverty schools, is clear, concise, and consistent. The instruction must be full of rigor that allows for ultimate inclusion and appreciation of innate abilities and immediate surroundings so as not to disproportionately label the behaviors of children living in poverty as detractors to the learning environment. Instead, their innate abilities and immediate surroundings should be harnessed and viewed as the panacea to the learning environment. "The subject-matter of the curriculum, however important, however judiciously selected, is empty of conclusive moral content until it is made over in terms of the individual's own activities, habits, and desires" (Dewey, 1909, p. 48).

To bring Dewey's statement into fruition, a principal's leadership must extend past the school walls and his or her influence must extend past that of curricular and budgetary matters. The principal must take on social/ communal matters that impact student achievement. Principals must be intrinsically involved in creating a true community of learners. Socio-Cultural Leadership's position on community leadership is articulated next.

Chapter 3

The Principal as the Leader of the Community

Decker and Decker (2003) provided Socio-Cultural Leadership with directional framework that separated the school community into two segments: the internal community and the external community. Bolman and Deal (1997), by way of their creation of the Human Resource Frame and the Political Frame, along with other researchers, offer key assumptions and values that combine to create principals' communal responsibilities under Socio-Cultural Leadership. The internal community, its impact on student achievement, and its relationship to Socio-Cultural Leadership will be explored first.

The internal community refers to school personnel, instructional and non-instructional. These people are administrators, teachers, teacher-leaders, counselors, social workers, paraprofessionals, clerical people, maintenance workers, and food service personnel. While their job descriptions are different, the principal must facilitate a process where they all work in unison toward a common goal, student achievement. Specifically, teachers must feel that (a) they are in a reciprocal relationship with the school (organizational reciprocity); (b) they are encouraged and expected to assume roles of leadership (teacher leadership); and (c) they are active participants in the decision making process (shared decision-making). Organizational reciprocity, teacher leadership, and shared decision making will be looked at separately in the following sections as the undercurrent of the Socio-Cultural Leader's understanding of the internal community.

Organizational Reciprocity

Organizational reciprocity is developed from Bolman and Deal's (1997) work on the Human Resource Frame. The Human Resource Frame does a more than adequate job of outlining the importance of synergy between an organization and the people that are employed by an organization. Primary assumptions about this frame are as follows: organizations are dependent on people; people are dependant on organizations; a good fit between organization and employee will yield positive results for both entities; likewise, a less than desirable fit will lead to organizational inefficiency and personal dissatisfaction.

School leaders must practice due diligence in ensuring that all employees feel that they significantly contribute to the primary goals of the school. Additionally, school leaders absolutely must make sure employees are getting what they desire out of the school as well. For some, what they need may be as little as job security or a steady, protected income. The will for an individual to pursue a career where below average financial compensation is the norm, is offset by the stability and safety of the career. "My salary may not be much, but at least I know it will be there," said one educator to me. I personally take offense when public opinions chastise teachers, especially, for not caring about students and only being in it for the money. Principals, please do not fall into this misguided way of thinking. A teacher, or any other employee, is not deserving of criticism just because they are driven by income and not by emotional commitment to the task. Instead, simply institute standards and accountability measures to fill the void of commitment to children. If financial security is the primary motivator for an employee, school leaders must reinforce the safeness of their income in exchange, of course, for quality performance.

On the other hand, teachers are also moved by being part of something big. They are moved by reaching out to the unreachable child. They are emotionally committed to children. Not only are they not in it for the money, they can often be found contributing what little personal resources they have back into the school. The Socio-Cultural Leader believes that teachers, and all other members of the internal community, make up the overwhelming majority of the workforce in education. Organizational reciprocity for these members of the internal community simply means reinforcing the fact that they are a part of something big and morally driven.

What can a leader give as remuneration to an individual for an investment of personal resources? Give these people respect. Give these people as much autonomy as possible. Give these people room to be creative and innovative. Believe it or not, this will mean more than a 3 percent raise that is only going to go towards taxes or gas.

Organizational reciprocity also means the preservation of democratic principles in managing the school. "Darling-Hammond (1997) found that schools that have restructured to function democratically produce high achievement with more students of all abilities and graduate more of them with better levels of skills and understanding than traditional schools do" (Brown and Anfara 2003, p. 22). Bolman and Deal (1997) concur in saying, "when the fit between people and organizations is poor, one or both suffers: individuals may feel neglected or oppressed, and organizations sputter because individuals withdraw their efforts or even work against organizational purposes" (p. 119).

In order to maximize student achievement, the principal must make sure that all members of the internal community are made to feel like equal communal stakeholders. Again, people must be made to feel that they own tiny pieces of the school. "Community membership can contribute to an individual's self-image and can bring about a certain kind of competence, self-confidence and empowerment" (Collins 2000, p. 165).

"The principal's role in defining the mission involves framing school wide goals and communicating these goals in a persistent fashion to the entire school community" (Hallinger and Murphy 1985, p. 221). It will be less of a challenge to show teachers how they contribute to increased student achievement. For many teachers, this is an obvious point. In a not so obvious manner, the principal must convince non-instructional members of the staff that students perform better in a school that is clean and safe. They must be convinced that students perform better when they receive contributions to a healthy diet from school. Last, but certainly not least, they must be convinced that a parent is more likely to support the direction of the school when their telephone calls to the school are received in a respectful manner. The point here is that while teachers are on the front lines of the instruction that takes place in a school, non-instructional members of the staff are on the front lines when it comes to the relationship between the internal community and the external community. Parents and students will often come into contact with the services of a clerical person, a facility service person, or a food service person, long before they come into contact with a teacher, counselor, or principal. In explicit terms, our non-instructional members of school staffs must know how valuable they are to student achievement.

Teacher Leadership

Acts of leadership must be evident in a variety of people within schools. "You cannot have highly effective principals unless there is distributive leadership throughout the school" (Fullan, 2003, p. 24). Typically, principals are former teachers. However, most principals are more than a decade away from the realities of the classroom. And, especially at the secondary level, the principal's instructional expertise is limited to one particular subject and/or one particular sub-topic of a subject.

A principal who is a former math teacher may have only taught algebra so he or she may be less than competent in providing direction in the areas of geometry and calculus. A principal who is a former social studies teacher may have only taught American History, making him or her not the best person to provide curricular direction to people who teach world history, geography, or economics. In addition, very, very few principals managed a classroom under the same societal pressures, mentioned in earlier chapters, that today's classroom teacher must negotiate. For the above mentioned reasons, if a principal's operational platform is not highly influenced by teachers, the academic experts, student achievement will not prosper.

> Wayson (1979) (as cited in Greenfield, 2004, p. 179) says a principal who wants to lead must learn how to facilitate... The principal should create conditions that will elicit leadership behaviors from everyone in the building in circumstances and at times that their contribution is essential for achieving the school's purpose.

Senge (1990) encouraged organizational leaders to create learning communities as a way to increase organizational output. Zepeda (2004) found that principals who encouraged teacher leadership were more successful at creating learning communities. "The principal had to relinquish top-down control and give the green light to teachers to move forward in their own learning—by creating and crafting new ways to achieve growth and renewal" (p. 151). The relinquishment of top-down control is an ideology that is often difficult for principals to embrace, as they are often publicly and privately challenged to take control.

> Educational leadership as a practice is caught inside the tensions created by the cultural images and power of having to be perceived publicly as a strong leader, while intellectually and morally recognizing the worth of others, inside and outside of schools. (Bogotch 2002, p. 154)

As a matter of fact, as principals attempt to transform school cultures being faced with new challenges, they will be dependent on the skill-flexibility of teachers. In a quantitative multi-national study, Rosenblatt (2004) found that teachers tended to be more skill-flexible when they had a role in the change, and less skill-flexible when school management initiated change or when change involved administrative objectives, as opposed to educational or social ones. Teachers also tended to be more skill-flexible when they believed that change had a positive impact on their work life, professional development, and student learning.

"Successful school reform involves a shift from controlling and directing at the top level to guiding and facilitating at all the levels" (Brown and Anfara, 2003, p. 23). This shift will be aided as teacher leadership is encouraged by the principal. "When teachers become leaders, principals will have more time to lead and more opportunities to follow" (Chirichello, 2004, p. 122).

Shared Decision Making

Waters, Marzano, and McNulty (2003) identified 21 leadership responsibilities most closely associated with improved student learning, two of which are (a) the willingness of the principal to challenge the status quo; and (b) the extent to which principals involve teachers in shared decision making (Yep and Chrispeels 2004, p. 4). The latter provides the focus of how shared decision making relates to Socio-Cultural Leadership.

It is not the will of the principal that serves as the only barrier to shared-decision making. Instead, principals often question the capacity of individuals to assume positions of influence. "Developing the capacity of individuals and staff members to engage in meaningful reform and restructuring to benefit students continues to be the challenge for school leaders" (Huffman 2003, p. 21). "By defying their isolation and working in groups, teachers can develop teams and increase their capacity for leadership" (Chirichello 2004, p. 122).

The benefit of shared decision-making will begin to truly shape learning gains in positive ways once capacity building is seen as a vital role in school leadership along with the creation of a forum for radical thinking. This forum for radical thinking is to be brought about by the principal.

> The ongoing leadership challenge is to create social and political spaces for advocates as well as outlaws to function inside and outside of schools and to deliberately encourage activists and radical intellectuals to make explicit the connections to their subjective meanings of social justice. (Bogotch 2002, p. 153)

The word *radical* is used to describe reformed thinking essential to school reform because of the transformation that communities in this country have gone through by way of cultural, religious, and ethnic diversification. Tyack (1974) synthesized this notion from a historical perspective of schooling in America. "But as villages grew into congested, heterogeneous cities, as conflicting values and strangers on the streets threatened the old pattern of Protestant socialization, decentralized decision making and pedagogical variety struck many educational leaders as anarchy" (p. 39).

Radical ways of reforming schools, if seen as a product of members of the internal community, are more effective at transforming school cultures than reform strategies that derive from isolated, individualized forms of leadership. "Successful teachers as leaders are adept at influencing constituencies over which they have no formal authority" (Bowman 2004, p. 187).

The literature on school leadership is careful not to suggest that shared-decision making alone instead of principal leadership will, by itself, lead to increased student achievement. In fact, using survey data from 1,762 teachers and 9,941 students, Leithwood and Jantzi (1999) found that there are greater effects of principal as opposed to teacher sources of leadership on student engagement, which is seen as a primary contributor on student achievement. Therefore the literature encourages a synergistic model where principal leadership and shared decision-making are evident, in unison, to foster student achievement. Fullan (2003) offers the following advice to bring together the tenets of strong individual leadership and shared decision-making.

> The environment cannot be improved only from the top. The top can provide a vision, policy incentives, mechanisms for interaction, coordination, and monitoring, but, to realize this vision, there must be lateral development—that

is, people at one's own level giving and receiving help across schools. (p. 47)

Again, the communal responsibilities of the principal, according to the tenets of Socio-Cultural Leadership, calls for principals to lead a charge where the internal and external community is poised for activities that will lend themselves to increased student achievement. Aforementioned sections on organizational reciprocity, teacher leadership, and shared decision-making summarized the relationship of the internal community on student achievement. The following section will look at the literature on the external community's impact on student achievement, especially in communities where high rates of children living in poverty reside.

The External Community

The external community consists of those persons not employed by the school, but with a vested interest in the product of public education. The external community also includes people with information and expertise that correlate with school reform. These people are parents, family members, business owners, residents, homeowners, members of the clergy, school boards, and politicians. The African proverb, "It takes a village to raise a child," alludes to the positive contributions that these people can place on the success rate of children.

In communities of high poverty especially, the activity and/or the inactivity of the external community creates the context that the internal community will have to manage. As teachers were the primary people that a principal must consider in the internal community, parents and family members are crucial to the school reform efforts in communities of high poverty. "Parents and families are among the most important influences on children's academic performance, particularly in families most at risk for school failure based on poverty" (Kitano 2003, p. 298).

Principals must be the catalyst for professional dialogue in schools; the type of dialogue that creates sensitivity to the dilapidated family structure that has become unfortunately prevalent for families living in poverty. This is to be done so that curriculum can begin to create stronger school-family ties. Additionally, school-wide efforts can begin to share information with families in nontraditional ways in order to maximize parental involvement in the educational process.

Governmental school reform initiatives, because of their technical language and use of academic jargon, will not realize the intent of these movements if extra emphasis is not placed on creating an understanding in the minds of community members. "Realizing and valuing community support and ideas is a crucial first step in a school's commitment to improving learning for all students" (Villa 2003, p. 777). The school, under the principal's leadership, has the duty of informing parents, especially parents living in poverty, of the newly developed expectations being placed on their children so that they can begin to join forces with the internal community. "Parents who understand and support educational standards will help their children meet these expectations" (Cunningham 2004, p. 33).

A U.S. Department of Education report stated that the most high-performing schools serving economically disadvantaged children distinguish themselves by finding innovative ways to connect with parents and private-sector partners (Sanders and Harvey 2002). "So many children today—and not just poor children—come from chaotic and unpredictable homes. Order in school gives them the stability and structure they need" (Checkley 2004, p. 71).

In order for the internal school community to truly encompass factors of the external community into the school culture, the "hidden rules" of poverty need to be addressed. Three of the hidden rules of poverty are, "the noise level is high (the TV is always on and everyone may talk at once), the most important information is non-verbal, and one of the main values of an individual is the ability to entertain" (Payne 1998, p. 18). Socio-Cultural Leadership does not bring up these hidden rules to suggest that educators accept them and excuse children when these hidden rules manifest themselves into disruptions to the learning environment. Nor, are these students to be systemically alienated from classrooms and schools. Principals must ensure that children who display anti-social behaviors, according to middle-class values, are reminded of acceptable social norms as part of the educational process. In other words, behavioral expectations are to remain high; the assistance we provide children in meeting these expectations is to remain even higher.

The internal community, made up of mainly people with middle-class values of education and a detachment of poverty-related characteristics, must also realize that economically disadvantaged communities sometimes have a decreased value of education. This detachment has been caused, in part, by "making it" in the eyes of lower socio-economic people being defined as leaving the poor community. "Wilson (1987) focuses on the role of class, and suggests that low-income residents of central city areas misperceive the benefits of schooling due to an exodus of middle-class families from urban centers beginning in the 1960s" (Ludwig, 1999, p. 18). The literature on school leadership points out that traditional school leadership philosophies do not adequately prepare principals for these transformed responsibilities of community building. Doyle (2004) gives an understanding of this phenomenon.

> Since the field of educational leadership was built on a foundation of organization and management theory, leadership for community building is not simply a change in language; it is a profound challenge for all educators to radically shift how they think and act. (p. 196)

"School community participants need to be involved in planning, coordinating, obtaining, and allocating resources such as time and money" (Doyle 2004, p. 198). This is possible if, and only if, principals reach out to the external community and create stronger ties between the internal and external communities.

> Creating stronger ties with families is accomplished by keeping parents informed about their children's progress and what they are learning, explaining how they can help children budget their time for homework assignments, and describing ways they can assist them with their school work. (Cunningham 2004, p. 35)

In addition, stronger ties with the external community will happen if the principal is aware of, and increases the internal community's awareness of, the chaotic family structure that is disproportionately evident in poverty-stricken environments. "In poverty, the roles, the multiple relationships, the nature of the male identity, the ever-changing allegiances, the favoritism, and the matriarchal structure result in a different pattern" (Payne 1998, p. 75). In accommodating alternative family structures, the principal must provide for new and enhanced ways of communicating with economically challenged single mothers, chiefly, as they are the ones most likely to be a mainstay in the lives of poor children. "Poor single mothers frequently experience interactions with school staff as intimidating, if not disrespectful and insulting" (Bloom 2003, p. 300). Under the principal's leadership, the internal community must have its sensitivity increased to this fact.

The principal should definitely add topics around social class to the professional dialogue in schools. As far as communication is concerned, the school must also examine the often ineffective communicative efforts used to converse with children of poverty. "To communicate is to give or exchange information; to have a meaningful relationship; to be connected" (Villa 2003, p. 778). Because of the alternative forms of family structure in poor communities alluded to earlier, there is extra need for improved school-student communication.

> One of the biggest issues with students from poverty is the fact that many children in poverty must function as their own parents. . . . In many instances they also act as parent to the adult in the household. . . . Educators tend to speak to students in a parent voice, particularly in discipline situations. . . . To the student who is already functioning as a parent, this is unbearable. . . .When the parent voice is used with a student who is already a parent in many ways, the outcome is anger. (Payne 1998, p. 106)

To support this concern, Peacock, McClure, and Agars (2003) found that weak parent-child attachment bonds are linked to a multiplicity of adolescent delinquent behaviors, including drug use, violent behaviors, and problems at school.

Chapter 4

The Principal as the Emotional Leader

In recent history, lead educational practitioners have called for the use of data as the driving force behind educational reform efforts. That said, these same people have all but ignored the profound data that exists regarding human thoughts and behaviors. In short, human feelings have been set aside in favor of overrated, unrealistic promises of technology-laced instructional programs and/or operational structures. "For several decades, educators seeking to introduce meaningful change have ignored much of the wisdom of educational philosophers and focused on programs than on people, more on reforms than on relationships" (Shields 2004, p. 114).

An unintended result of most educational reform strategies at all levels (federal, state, and local) has been the lessening of efficacy in the hearts and minds of teachers, students, parents, and principals. In keeping with the thematic structure of this book, this is especially true in communities where there exists a high rate of students living in poverty. The lack of belief that these citizens feel is surmounted only by their lack of confidence in school and/or community leaders in addressing their concerns.

Those persons within school communities, internal and external, that wish to be a part of effective school reform for children living in poverty are often in a thorny emotional state because of the seemingly insurmountable obstacles that they face and the lack of self-efficacy that exists to diminish these obstacles. It becomes the Socio-Cultural Leader's bounded duty to foster productive interpersonal relationships between all members of the community as a means towards increased student achievement. Fullan (2001) cited the building of interpersonal relationships as the second most important function of an organizational leader.

To combat feelings of inadequacy alluded to earlier and to build key relationships within a school, principals must be skilled in emotional intelligence. Principals must generate emotional commitments, and feelings of resolve, in the hearts and minds of people that are to impact student achievement.

While many theorists have contributed to the literature on emotional intelligence, there is not one single definition of it. Instead, we are left to the interpretations and assumptions of a variety of theorists.

> In the specific instance of emotions and leadership, Humphrey (2002) argued that leadership is intrinsically an emotional process through which leaders recognize employees' emotional states, attempt to evoke emotions in employees, and then seek to manage employees' emotional states accordingly. (Askanasy & Dasborough 2003, p. 19)

Emotional Competencies for School Leaders

Goleman (2002), arguably the contemporary expert on emotional intelligence, offers a comprehensive set of leadership competencies for the emotionally intelligent leader. As a catalyst, this component of Socio-Cultural Leadership makes use of Goleman's work, meant for leaders of all types of organizations, and provides examples specific to the educational leader, primarily the principal of a school.

Emotional self-awareness. *Leaders high in emotional self-awareness are attuned to their inner signals, recognizing how their feelings affect them and their job performance.* Unless a principal in a high poverty school truly believes in the notion that all children can learn and demonstrate academic proficiency, he or she will constantly remain at a disadvantage in terms of leading reform efforts. A leader's true feelings will become transparent to his or her community. One must keep in mind that a school's community will take on the personality, and the belief system, of the leader.

Accurate self-assessment. *Leaders who regularly self-assess typically know their limitations and strengths, and exhibit a sense of humor about them.* Nothing is worse than a school principal who is not aware of his or her strengths and weaknesses. It is imperative that a principal who has a proven track record of being an effective school leader from an operational perspective, not attempt to impose too much will on curriculum and instruction. The opposite is also true. They key here is for the principal to surround herself with people who have skill sets that are supplemental to her own.

Self-confidence. *Knowing their abilities with accuracy allows leaders to play to their strengths. Such leaders often have a sense of presence, a self-assurance that lets them stand out in a group.* Have you ever seen someone walk into a room and command instant respect without saying or doing anything? I have. Often, true leadership has a certain walk, a certain talk, a certain air, and a certain swagger. Keep in mind that there is a fine line that exists between confidence that builds followership and arrogance that serves to foster alienation.

Self-control. *Leaders with emotional self-control find ways to manage their disturbing emotions and impulses, and even channel them in useful ways.* In organizations, there is a natural tendency for crap to role downhill. The principal, especially in a low-performing, high-poverty school, will often be the subject of extreme critique and doubt. The Socio-Cultural Leader will shoulder this ridicule, at times brutal, without passing it on to teachers. Why? If we, educational leaders, allow crap to role downhill without ever stopping it, guess who is at the bottom of the hill? Students.

Transparency. *Leaders who are transparent live their values. Transparency—an authentic openness to others about one's feelings, beliefs, and actions—allows integrity.* A principal must have a belief system that reflects the notion that all children can learn and it is the primary responsibility of the school to make this happen. In addition, the principal must make use of every opportunity to articulate these beliefs verbally. It must not stop there. The principal must also ensure that all actions and decisions are consistent with this belief.

Adaptability. *Leaders who are adaptable can juggle multiple demands without loosing their focus or energy, and are comfortable with the inevitable ambiguities of organizational life.* The average principal will be called upon to serve as an accountant, an architect, a contractor, a physician, an attorney, and a teacher. The principal will have tasks to complete that are aligned with these professions and he will have to complete them within a timeframe that would make the most structured individual apprehensive. Such is the life of a principal.

Achievement. *Leaders with strength in achievement have high personal standards that drive them to constantly seek performance improvements—both for themselves and those they lead.* It can be stated that a principal's primary job is to manage the acquisition of intellect. The principal cannot meet this responsibility unless he or she possess a high rate of intellect and is always seeking more. The leader of a learning institution should be just that, the lead learner.

Initiative. *Leaders who have a sense of efficacy—that they have what it takes to control their own destiny—excel in initiative. They seize opportunities—or create them—rather than simply waiting.* Instead of using ambiguous terminology in local, state, and federal reform directives as reasons why students cannot learn, a principal must seize the opportunity to collaboratively create solutions with, and for, the local community. Vague and/or unfunded expectations in governmental reform initiatives should be viewed as an opportunity for local leadership to thrive.

Optimism. *A leader who is optimistic can roll with the punches, seeing an opportunity rather than a threat in a setback.* One principal uses the fact that the school district has just undergone massive budget cuts as the reason why additional instructional materials cannot be purchased and subsequently why student achievement cannot improve. Another principal rallies the teachers around their own instructional and curricular expertise, assembles them into learning communities, and convinces them that they can create supplemental academic activities for their students in order to enrich student learning. Which principal exhibits optimism? Which principal improves achievement?

Empathy. *Leaders with empathy are able to attune to a wide range of emotional signals, letting them sense the felt, but unspoken, emotions in a person or group.* Teachers work long, frustrating hours and are inadequately financially compensated. That said, they often use personal time and money to increase the likelihood of student learning. The empathetic principal realizes these facts and creates ways of acknowledging them. Understanding if a teacher is a little late to work, allowing a teacher to use an occasional planning period to take care of personal business, and offering to cover a teacher's class while a potty break is taken, are all ways that principals can demonstrate a little empathy.

Organizational awareness. *A leader with a keen social awareness can be politically astute, able to detect crucial social networks and read key power relationships.* Within a school, there are often formal and informal social networks of like-minded people. These networks are usually chaired by an individual. In order to effectively establish and make use of two-way communicative efforts in a school, the principal will need to know that these networks exist and become one with their structures.

Service. *Leaders high in the service competence foster an emotional climate so that people directly in touch with the customer or client will keep the relationship on the right track.* Teachers need to feel that they are held accountable to the educational needs of children. For this to happen, principals must establish a school climate where they are held accountable to meet the operational needs of the teacher. Plainly put, if principals dedicate themselves to servicing teachers, students stand a better chance of getting serviced by teachers.

Inspiration. *Leaders who inspire both create resonance and move people with a compelling vision or shared mission.* Similar to the pedagogical push to add rigor to instruction because students are not stimulated when the bar is set too low, is the need for school principals to provide the same level of rigor to teachers. Principals must be the local catalysts to a movement that involves teachers in tackling student achievement from a global perspective. When principals simply demand improved test scores from teachers, they have in effect set the bar too low to inspire authentic participation from teachers. However, when principals convince teachers that their primary mission should be to create a more literate child that can use reason and logic to improve the economic conditions of an entire commune, rigor has been added to the expectations of teachers. Their hearts and minds will soon follow.

Influence. *Indicators of a leader's power of influence range from finding just the right appeal for a given listener to knowing how to build buy-in from key people and a network of support for an initiative.* A principal wishing to institute any kind of operational and/or instructional change in a school should employ facts and figures in order to generate teacher buy-in. A principal should utilize salesmanship skills in order to generate teacher buy-in. A principal should make use of a pre-existing interpersonal, emotional bond with teachers in order to generate buy-in. Autocratic directives, laced with consequences for non-compliance, should be used as a last resort to generate teacher buy-in; while realizing that this tactic will not yield optimal levels of teacher buy-in.

Developing others. *Leaders who are adept at cultivating people's abilities show a genuine interest in those they are helping along, understanding their goals, strengths and weaknesses.* It is a declaration of Socio-Cultural Leadership that leadership development is just that, leadership development. If I walk into a school and I see the principal making all of the decisions and taking care of all of the managerial operational needs of a school, the first question I ask myself is who is fulfilling the role of the principal? Who is coaching? Who is mentoring? Who is establishing and monitoring the collaborative vision? Principals that lead followers will fall substantially short of principals that lead leaders in the student achievement race.

Change catalyst. *Leaders who can catalyze change are able to recognize the need for change, challenge the status quo, and champion the new order.* Principals must exhibit the type of effective, courageous, and critical leadership that it takes to lead people to the top of mountain and have the wherewithal to look out over the valley and convince people that they have climbed the wrong mountain. This type of principal will generate just as much, if not more, commitment from teachers on the second mountain as the first.

Conflict management. *Leaders who manage conflicts best are able to draw out all parties, understand the differing perspectives, and then find a common ideal that everyone can endorse.* Conflict is certain to emerge in schools, especially in schools that serve high rates of children living in poverty. Principals should not avoid conflict. Conflict should be sought out, positively and creatively confronted, and used as the foundation to create common meaning and direction. If teachers differ on which instructional strategy is more effective, the energy that is driving their feelings can and should be used to create a better educational environment for children. Do not, as so many principals have done, merely dismiss the conflict in favor of mandated, top-down, pedagogical requirements. Merely giving in to the resistance is not progressive principal behavior either.

Teamwork and Collaboration. *Leaders who are able team players generate an atmosphere of friendly collegiality and are themselves models of respect, helpfulness, and cooperation.* Plainly put, happy, respected, empowered, supported, informed teachers will create better learning environments. A school is like a sandbox. It would behoove a principal to play nicely with the people who share his or her sandbox.

The previously stated adaptive use of Goleman's competencies (Goleman, 2002, p. 253), provide the Socio-Cultural Leader with a glimpse of how emotional intelligence will lead to greater worker productivity, community input, and ultimately student achievement and well-being.

Results from the Research on Emotional Intelligence

Over the last decade, many studies have been conducted that demonstrate a strong correlation between emotional intelligence and organizational performance and/or the performance of individuals within an organization.

Using 144 second-year undergraduate students as participants at an Australian university, Askanasy and Dasborough (2003) found that an interest in and knowledge of emotional intelligence (EQ) of teammates predicted team performance. In a similar study, Wong and Law (2002) found that the emotional intelligence of leaders was associated with increased employee job satisfaction and "extra-role" behaviors (p. 19). Most teachers, especially high-performing teachers, work two shifts every day. The first shift is used to teach and supervise children. This is the shift that they are paid to work. The second shift, once children go home, is the shift used to return parent phone calls, grade papers, create lesson plans, collaborate with colleagues, and attend professional development seminars. These are all examples of the extra-role behaviors that comprise the second shift—the shift that teachers are NOT paid to work. Needless to say, the emotionally intelligent principal is more likely to have teachers who are more willing to work the ever so needed second shift.

In a study that spanned 40 years, Feist and Barron (1996), using 80 PhDs, found that social and emotional abilities were four times more important than IQ in determining professional success and prestige. In an analysis of job competencies of 286 international organizations, Spencer and Spencer (1993) found that 18 of 21 competencies used to differentiate superior from average performers were related to EQ.

In a longitudinal study that compared cognitive and emotional competencies' impact on an individual's work performance gauged by promotion, Dulewicz and Higgs (1998) found that EQ contributes more to career advancement than does IQ. In an article in *Time* (1995), "The EQ Factor," the author proposed that while IQ may get one hired, EQ is more likely to get one promoted.

"Starratt (1995) reminds educators that the real source of the leader's power is not in the person or the position, it is in the vision that attracts the commitment and enthusiasm of members" (Brown and Anfara 2003, p. 28). There are teachers out there who have the uncanny ability to generate unbelievably high levels of respect and compliance from students; all students, especially at-risk students. Likewise, there are some teachers who cannot generate the most basic level of compliance from the most cooperative group of children. This finding is due to the interpersonal connection that exists between teachers and students. Surprisingly, or maybe not, this phenomena is also found in the principal-teacher relationship. Some principals can get a group of teachers to create a school-wide curriculum focus calendar and collaboratively decide on instructional strategies, based on the needs of the students, which will yield most favorable results. In contrast, some principals find it difficult to impossible to get 100 percent attendance at monthly faculty meetings. What is the difference you ask? Some principals have *it* and some principals do not. *It* is an interpersonal relationship with teachers filled with optimism, empathy, service, and high expectations.

In order to bring theoretical constructs of emotional intelligence into fruition, school leaders require practical advice in being able to demonstrate concern for teachers. In this regard, there is no shortage of advice for principals from the literature. "A principal demonstrates individual concern when she or he approaches each teacher individually with respect and fairness; is accessible to teachers; supports, encourages, and recognizes individual efforts; and provides direction and guidance based on individual needs and development" (Barnett and McCormick 2004, p. 429). Leithwood, Steinbach, and Jantzi (2002) offer additional direction for principals in this regard. "School leaders contribute to the positive valence of teachers' emotions by complimenting teachers on good work, requesting their advice on important matters, and ensuring that others inside and outside the school are aware of teachers' contributions to the success of the school" (p. 103).

The first three domains of Socio-Cultural Leadership (instructional, community, and emotional) reflect leadership traits that, in and of themselves, can predict student achievement outcomes. The literature on school leadership is also overwhelmed with information that suggests that a leader's behavior, and its relationship to student achievement, may be heavily moderated by that of the culture of a school. That being the case, the cultural domain of Socio-Cultural Leadership seeks to raise the consciousness of principals to (a) the impact of school culture, (b) recognize the nuances of organizational change, (c) and the interwoven relationship of both.

Chapter 5

The Principal as the Facilitator of School Culture

Next to the quality of instruction, principal leadership is often thought to be the most significant factor to influence student learning outcomes in a school. This is certainly the sentiment of the first three domains (instructional, community, and emotional) of Socio-Cultural Leadership. However, Witziers, Bosker, and Kruger (2003) found, via a quantitative meta-analysis between 1986 and 1996, very small positive effects linking leadership with student achievement. These findings confirm earlier research findings that suggest culture is more of a predictor of organizational success than leadership. "For it is culture, the powerful socializer of thought and programmer of behavior" (Sergiovanni 1992, p. 95) that strongly influences achievement, morale, and connectedness in our schools" (Fiore 2000, p. 11).

To think that there is something more influential on student achievement than leadership, and to suggest that the something is school culture is definitely reflective of radical thinking. As radical as it may be, the matter is more than deserving of additional exploration. Throughout my research, it was very difficult to find much on school culture. My take is that it is not widely studied because it is an abstract concept and therefore it is not widely understood. That said, researchers and practitioners are in need of common language when speaking of school culture.

Culture Defined

To say that there are vast and varied meanings of school/organizational culture, would be an understatement. While Leithwood and Jantzi (1999) defined organizational culture as the norms, values, beliefs, and assumptions that shape members' decisions and practices, there are a number of additional definitions of culture that follow:

- According to Bates (1992), culture is "the framework that connects beliefs, values, and knowledge with action" (p. 98).
- Weaver (1996) defines school culture as the general pattern of interactions between the internal and the external community.
- Schein (1985) defines culture as a system of ordinary meaning and symbols that is learned and shared among members of a naturally bounded social group (as cited in Gruenert 1998).
- "A pattern of shared basic assumptions that the group has learned as it solved its problems of external adaptation and internal integration, that has worked well enough to be considered valid and, therefore, to be taught to new members as the correct way to perceive, think, and feel in relation to those problems" (Schein 1992, p. 12).
- Culture refers "to the guiding beliefs and expectations evident in the way a school operates, particularly in reference to how people relate (or fail to relate) to each other" (Fullan and Hargreaves 1996, p. 37).
- Bruner (1996) offers a humanistic approach to understanding school culture. "Culture is all about a mode of coping with human problems; with human transactions of all sorts, depicted in symbols" (p. 99).
- Hofstede (1997) defines school culture by group membership. "Culture is defined as the collective programming of the mind which distinguishes the members of one group or category of people from another" (p. 180).

Morey and Luthans (1985) (as cited in Gruenert 1998) outline the following facets of organizational culture that is pertinent to the topic:

- Culture is learned; it is not genetic or biological.
- Culture is shared by people as members of social groups.
- Culture is transgenerational and cumulative in its development.
- Culture is symbolic in that it is based on the human capacity to create symbols.

- Culture is patterned; it is organized and integrated.
- Culture is adaptive; it is the basic human adaptive mechanism.

Plainly stated, culture is defined as "the way we do things around here." To illustrate this, consider the following as an excerpt from a conversation that a veteran teacher has with a novice teacher upon the novice teacher's arrival on the faculty.

> *Around here*, we (teachers) are expected to collaboratively decide what is important for students to learn. *Around here*, we are expected to then collaboratively decide how we will know when students have mastered the intended curriculum. *Around here*, we then collaboratively decide how to intervene when some students fail to master the intended curriculum. Finally, *around here*, we are expected to collaboratively decide how we will enrich the learning experiences of those students who have proven mastery of the intended curriculum. *Around here*, not only are these expectations of your superiors (principals and assistant principals), these are the expectations of your colleagues (fellow teachers). *Around here*, if you are a secretary, or a custodian, or a cafeteria worker, you are expected to use your job functionalities in order to support these activities. *Around here*, this is just the way we do things.

For your own edification, compare a school where the above-mentioned activities are normative, generally expected behaviors of the internal community members. Now consider a school, where the opposites are true. Which school would you think has created the most optimal conditions for student learning?

Cultural Symbolism

The categorizations and definitions of school culture mentioned in the previous section, all in one way or another, symbolize organizational priorities and therefore dictate organizational success, or lack thereof. Bolman and Deal (1997) synthesized symbolic organizational happenings into what they called the *Symbolic Frame*. All organizations exist to achieve certain goals and to create specific perceptions in the minds of their constituents. This is done so that the organization can attract people that will permeate these goals and perceptions.

While an organization's beliefs are complex and subject to constant change, they must be articulated to people via simplified, easy to follow pieces of information. This is where the Symbolic Frame comes in. "Symbols embody and express an organization's culture—the interwoven pattern of beliefs, values, practices, and artifacts that define for members who they are and how they are to do things" (Bolman and Deal 1997, p. 217). Symbols are the most efficient way that an organization's character and culture are communicated.

Symbols can be expressed through a number of different avenues. Myths, stories, rituals, and ceremonies, as presented in Bolman and Deal's (1997) Symbolic Frame, are excellent examples.

- Myths, like all other symbols, will expose positive and negative things about an organization. "They communicate unconscious wishes and conflicts" (p. 220). In addition, "myths arise to protect people from uncertainty, but they are not intended to be empirically testable" (p. 254). A commonly shared myth can support progressive ideologies. "At the same time, myths are stubbornly persistent, potentially blocking adaptation to changing conditions" (p. 221).
- Stories can be entertaining, easy to remember excerpts of an organization's history used to share basic tenets. "Stories are a key medium for communicating corporate myths. They establish and perpetuate tradition" (p. 222). We need to keep in mind that symbolic stories change with the time and we should allow our mental models to change with them.
- Rituals have the potential to uncover a wide variety of observable happenings within an organization. They articulate an organizations culture by developing a pattern of beliefs, values, practices, and artifacts that assist members in navigation of local terrain. "In a school, rituals could be the daily taking of attendance, the faculty meetings every first Tuesday of the month, or reciting the Pledge of Allegiance each morning" (Gruenert 1998, p. 20).
- Ceremonies, according to Bolman and Deal (1997), exist to stabilize, to socialize, to reduce ambiguity, and to convey messages to nonmembers. They are normally infrequent occurrences yet major contributors to the culture of a school.

Within the *Symbolic Frame*, there is on-going controversy of the meaning of cultures in organizations. "Some people argue that organizations *have* culture; others insist that organizations *are* cultures" (p. 231). Both meanings are seen as having equivalent value.

Assessing School Culture

In schools, information gathered and assessed from teachers proves to be an accurate measure of school culture. Statements, made by teachers, such as, "Leaders value teachers' ideas;" "Leaders support risk-taking and innovation in teaching;" "Teachers are generally aware of what other teachers are teaching;" "Leaders take time to praise teachers that perform well;" and "Teachers are kept informed on current issues in the school;" if measured, will give insight into a school's culture *(Statements taken from Gruenert's School Culture Survey)*.

According to the research on school culture, repetitive practices among teachers and other members of the internal community manifest themselves into normative school behavior and greatly influence school outcomes, i.e. student achievement. "To influence the practices of their colleagues, therefore, school leaders often will have to influence the system of shared norms, values, and beliefs that (usually implicitly) shape their colleagues' interpretations of events" (Leithwood and Jantzi 1999, p. 683). How is this done? According to Witziers, Bosker, and Kruger (2003), "Principals should have high expectations of teachers and student achievement, supervise teachers, coordinate the curriculum, emphasize basic skills, and monitor student progress" (p. 401).

These regularly executed behaviors on the part of the principal will translate themselves into a school culture that is most advantageous to higher rates of student achievement, among children living in poverty especially. If there is found to be an ineffective school culture and/or the school is faced with increased expectations and less than favorable conditions (i.e., poverty), the principal must reshape school culture. The principal must be adept at creating and sustaining changes in a school's culture.

Change and Culture

Fullan (2001) and Evans (1996) (as cited in Gruenert 1998) both concur in saying that organizational culture will impact members' beliefs, attitudes, and behaviors in a manner that will, if it goes unnoticed, preserve the status quo and deter change efforts. Changes in schools include different emphasis in program of study, operational processes, fresh instructive programs, and an influx of students and teachers with assorted social backgrounds and conditions.

Relationships between teachers and students, and the assumptions teachers have regarding education are the two cultural changes that must happen in order for school improvement to take place. "To adjust effectively to such changes, schools need to be flexible, namely, be able to adjust to change" (Rosenblatt 2004, p. 1). "The leader's job is to help change context—to introduce new elements into the situation that are bound to influence behavior for the better" (Fullan 2003, p. 1).

Principals often find changing a school's culture to be an intricate task; primarily because of their aversion towards creating tension among members of the community. In the politically driven world context that principals, especially principals in low socio-economic communities, must contend with; the idea of intentionally creating communal dissension seems absurd. The reality is tension is a key component to change; especially momentous change. To prove this point, I once challenged a group of principals to think about all of the many attributes in twenty-first-century America that make them proud to be an American. Some of their answers included, but were not limited to, (a) abolishment of governmental endorsement of racism and segregation; (b) the entitlement that women have to vote; and (c) regardless of political opinion, an unconditional national appreciation for members of our military who are at war. I then challenged them to list all of the momentous changes in our country that did not stem from some type of controversy, some type of conflict among groups, and some type of widespread tension. I used their inability to create such a list to substantiate the need for tension as a vehicle for change.

"In order to initiate change within a culture, it is necessary to create tension, to build from conflict, and to increase the capacity of staff members to deal with ambiguity" (Gruenert 1998, p. 32). This is keen and valuable insight into the role of school leaders, as change is often a difficult process. While the process is difficult, principals must seek out opportunities to augment culture for the better, without allowing the potential chaos to serve as a deterrent. "Leaders in a culture of change value and almost enjoy the tensions inherent in addressing hard-to-solve problems because that is where the greatest accomplishments lie" (Fullan 2001, p. 8).

One would think that a principal's responsibility is to keep things calm, peaceful, and uneventful in a school. "The paradox is that transformation would not be possible without accompanying messiness" (Fullan 2001, p. 31). "Changing the culture of an organization is a difficult and time-consuming process that must have at its center the development and working knowledge of a vision shared by all stakeholders" (Huffman 2003, p. 22). Kotter (1996) confined organizational change into an eight-stage process:

1. Establish a sense of urgency.
2. Create the guiding coalition.
3. Develop a vision and strategy.
4. Communicate the change vision.
5. Empower employees for broad-based action.
6. Generate short-term wins.
7. Consolidate gains and produce more change.
8. Anchor new approaches in the culture (p. 21).

To suggest that creating sustainable cultural changes in a school that serves a high percentage of children living in poverty is challenging, would be putting it mildly. "Moving people, as leaders are called to do, can only happen when the followers see, understand, and truly believe in the leader" (Fiore 2000, p. 11). Also, while stability in the ranks of school leadership is often seen as an advantageous thing, it is less than plausible for a creator of current school culture to be the one to successfully augment a school's culture. What does this mean? "If you are the leader, and have been in that position for a significant period of time, and you perceive that the culture needs to change, go away, chances are that you are at least part of the problem and not the best person to lead to its solution" (Robbins and Finley 1997, p. 189).

Chapter 6

The Socio-Cultural Leadership Questionnaire (SCLQ)

Once I created Socio-Cultural Leadership, I decided that in today's data-driven world it would not be enough to simply create this model for school leadership. I felt that I needed to devise a way to quantify the existence of Socio-Cultural Leadership traits among principals. Commensurate with the current era of accountability, it was also determined that school boards and superintendents would have an interest in collecting this type of data in order to evaluate principal effectiveness and more importantly the extent at which "principal effectiveness" contributed to increased student achievement as measured by standardized tests. Lastly, as the *No Child Left Behind Act* called for the implementation of research-based school leadership practices for schools in need of restructuring, it seemed necessary to create a reliable and valid instrument of this nature.

In order to fulfill these ideals, I began a research study. For the edification of the reader, this chapter will outline the steps taken in my research study.

Overview of the Study

The conceptual framework of this study suggested that school culture must adopt a philosophy in support of the notion that public education is meant to serve the greater community and that effective leadership at all levels of the system, specifically the school principal level, is the only way that public education will fulfill its obligation to society. While the literature offered many aspects of effective school leadership, I realized that none were more substantial than: (a) as the instructional leader, the principal must supervise and evaluate instruction to make sure that students are given optimal learning opportunities; (b) as the emotional leader, the principal must ensure that teachers are intellectually equipped, emotionally stimulated, and encouraged to assume decision making positions of leadership in schools to increase student achievement; (c) as a community leader, the principal must inspire and/ or provide incentives for communal learning that is student-centered; and (d) as a school leader, the principal must also realize the limitations of leadership on student achievement and begin to shape, and continuously reshape, school culture, which may have more of an impact on student achievement than leadership.

After finding a void in the current literature of these theoretical themes, I used the above synthesis of school leadership theory to put together a distinct model of school leadership and subsequently named that model, Socio-Cultural Leadership. It was also conceptually proposed that the aforementioned four descriptors of Socio-Cultural Leadership (instructional, community, emotional, cultural) represented four uncorrelated domains of the model.

Then I sought to find what, if any, empirical evidence existed to suggest that principals in high-poverty schools demonstrated behavioral attributes of Socio-Cultural Leadership and what relationship existed between these behaviors and student achievement. Practically speaking, two events were measured and then compared: (a) the principals' leadership and (b) student achievement. The latter of the two was taken from student results on the Florida Comprehensive Assessment Test (FCAT) and the principals' leadership was determined by the perceptions of teachers who completed the Socio-Cultural Leadership Questionnaire (SCLQ).

A number of survey instruments have been developed to measure principal behaviors and attitudes thought to have a prevailing impact on school conditions, specifically student achievement (Lester and Bishop 2000), thus creating a sense of precedence for me to attempt to ascertain principal behaviors through instrumentation. While these survey instruments served as precedents for measuring principal effectiveness through quantitative measures, they failed to measure the essence of Socio-Cultural Leadership; thus necessitating the creation of the SCLQ.

In order to create the SCLQ, I (a) transformed theoretical findings from the literature into measurable constructs (variables/questions); (b) verified the theoretical relationships of the constructs with experts in the related fields of research; (c) generated feedback from non-sampled teachers on the readability of questions and structure of the instrument (pilot study); (d) statistically determined internal consistency of each of the four domains separately; and finally (e) used principal components analysis to explore the existence of the four domains as described.

To test the validity of the Socio-Cultural Leadership construct, a large urban school district was chosen as the contextual backdrop of this study. All K-12, high poverty schools (50 percent or more of the students participate in the Federal Free or Reduced Price Lunch Program) within the district that retained the same principal for two or more years were solicited for participation in this study. The FCAT, and the FCAT only, constituted student achievement. Personal demographic data (race, gender, religion, nationality, sexual orientation, etc) related to the principals were not used to include or exclude a school from the study. The respondents in this study were all urban school teachers in the above targeted schools. A total of 903 urban school teachers contributed to the study. The SCLQ used a Likert-type scale (A = Always, B = Often, C = Sometimes, D = Rarely, and E = Never) to depict responder answers. A cadre of statistical procedures was then used empirically to fulfill the intent of this study.

Major Findings and Conclusions

To reiterate, the primary purpose of this study was to establish the reliability and validity of the SCLQ. The version of the SCLQ administered to elementary and secondary teachers contained forty questions and were separated into the four hypothesized domains that comprise this model of school leadership (instructional, emotional, community, and cultural) as described in earlier chapters. The findings in this study explicitly provided substantive and empirical support for the leadership model, Socio-Cultural Leadership.

All four domains met the desired measure of internal consistency which was a Cronbach Alpha of .70 or higher and there were no high inter-item correlations; meaning that the hypothesized model actually measured the proposed theoretical constructs and enough evidence was derived to consider each item (question) as an independent variable within each domain.

While internal consistency of each domain was determined to be high, the principal components analysis did not find that Socio-Cultural Leadership was made up of four domains as hypothesized. Instead of four domains that were originally hypothesized, the statistical analysis found that there were actually five domains. Thus, the four original domains developed were composed of five independent and distinct components for the purpose of survey instrumentation.

The five distinct domains of the SCLQ derived from the statistical analysis were labeled as follows: (1) Interpersonal Leadership Traits (ILT) which accounted for 42.04 percent of the variance; (2) Outreach to Parents (OP) which accounted for 4.8 percent of the variance; (3) Measures of Accountability (MA) which accounted for 3.8 percent of the variance; (4) Communication of Instructional Priorities (CIP) which accounted for 2.8 percent of the variance; and (5) Management of Instructional Process Detractors (MIPD) which accounted for 2.5 percent of the variance. These five sections of the instrument, totaling 27 retained items and labeled because of the commonalities found in the questions that loaded high on each subscale, accounted for 56.20 percent of the variance explained by the original 40 item SCLQ. The overall reliability coefficients for the five derived domains were high and ranged from .883 (ILT) to .584 (MIPD).

It is more than understandable if the information stated above is a little confusing. In laymen's terms, the four theoretically determined domains of Socio-Cultural Leadership (instructional, emotional, community, and culture) can be empirically measured by using twenty-seven of the original forty questions. These twenty-seven questions are grouped into five sub-groups (interpersonal leadership traits, outreach to parents, measures of accountability, communication of instructional priorities, and management of instructional process detractors) on the survey instrument.

In addition, the twenty-seven items are effective in measuring 56.2 percent of the theoretical model Socio-Cultural Leadership. Practically speaking, it is essential that the most information possible is gleaned from the fewest number of questions on a survey instrument. Statistical research tells us that the more questions that respondents have to answer, lessens the potential for data that is absolutely reflective of the respondents' feelings.

As for the predictability of student achievement derived from the subscales of the SCLQ, OP (outreach to parents) and MIPD (management of instructional process detractors) positively correlated with student achievement (n = 903). This positive correlation was found to be significant at the $p < .01$ level, which was a Bonferroni adjustment of a .05 alpha level due to the testing of multiple hypothesizes.

Essentially, this study empirically proved that as principals exhibited behaviors depicted by subscales OP and MIPD, FCAT scores increased. The schools sampled were separated into two groups (high-performing and low-performing) based on their FCAT scores. Principals in high-performing schools exhibited behaviors indicated by subscales OP (outreach to parents) and MIPD (management of instructional process detractors) significantly more than principals in low-performing schools. Furthermore, these findings were correct at least 95 percent of the time and not caused by a Type I sampling error. While the entire twenty-seven-item SCLQ is correlated to student achievement, subscales OP and MIPD can be used to predict student achievement outcomes. The SCLQ is to be administered in its entirety.

Strengths of the Study

There were many strengths of this study that may contribute to the utility and generalizability of the findings; primarily in the areas of (a) review of literature; (b) contextual setting; and (c) sample size. As for the review of literature, more than 160 books, research studies, and peer-reviewed articles were consulted around the topics of school leadership, organizational leadership, school improvement, and poverty. The conceptual framework was significantly influenced by the discoveries of said body of literature. The large urban school district located in the south-eastern portion of the United States selected as the contextual backdrop of this study, made for an opportune setting to collect data from teachers who work with large concentrations of children living in poverty. The sampling of teachers that participated in this study (n = 903), statistically contributed to the significance in the findings of this study.

Weaknesses of the Study

As there are facts about the study that added to the utility of the findings, there are aspects of this study that threaten the generalizability of the findings, primarily in the areas of (a) methodology; (b) conceptual framework; and (c) number of districts sampled. This was an exploratory study based on the potential impact of a pre-determined conceptual framework derived from theory. Intuitively speaking, there is some tension in using exploratory analysis in attempting to confirm pre-established or hypothesized theory. While researcher objectivity in the analysis of research used to conceptualize the framework was vigorously pursued, researcher bias was still evident in the selection of literature and the selection of salient themes from the literature. This was only one study, in one district; therefore the findings may not be applicable in other settings without further statistical analysis.

Retrospective Alternatives to the Study

While the body of research used to conceptualize the initial four domains (instruction, emotion, community, culture) was robust, more steps could have been taken in order to refine the resulting questionnaire items. This study did one pilot study and only asked ninety-six teachers (83 percent responded) to comment on the readability of each question and the structure of the instrument. The teachers surveyed in the pilot study, were not urban school teachers and none were secondary; perhaps, they should have been.

Admittedly, I also ignored a salient theme from the pilot study respondents; which was to add a responder option of "Don't Know" to the Likert-type scaled used. Of the sample that completed the SCLQ (n = 903), there was a diminutive yet notable amount of missing answers. At the onset of this study, my assumption was that teachers had an awareness of the principal behaviors depicted by the questionnaire. This assumption rendered potentially valuable data missing from this study. Instead of noting missing values and replacing them with mean values, as I did, I could have given the respondents an opportunity to say, "I do not know" to a particular question. This would have added additional data to be analyzed.

A large urban school district was an appropriate locale for this study to take place; however not expanding this study to other districts, in other parts of the state and country, prevented the study from having heterogeneous significance in terms of geographical and cultural settings. In addition to having a more diverse number of districts participate in this study, I could have solidified the participation of one hundred percent of the schools that qualified instead of 26 percent. An increase in sample sizes of districts, schools, and teachers, would have enabled me to compare and contrast the findings of this study around further variables such as race, gender, class, grade level, and student exceptionalities; just to name a few.

Practical Implications for Principals and Author's Final Declaration

In summation, of the five subscales of the SCLQ, 2 of them, OP (outreach to parents) and MIPD (management of instructional process detractors), can predict student achievement. While the predictability of student achievement from these two subscales were significant and positive, they were low (.134 and .094 respectively). On the surface, one may suggest that predictability of student achievement cannot be made based on these data. That would be an immense mistake in judgment. With all of the many people and factors that contribute to student achievement outcomes, to empirically demonstrate that the attitudes and behaviors of one person, the principal, can predict student achievement at all, has mammoth implications for practicing principals, college level principal training programs, superintendents, and school boards.

The preceding study represented a four-year intellectual journey into principal leadership behaviors that contribute to increased student achievement; especially among students living in poverty. Ironically, the journey began with questions, and still it ended with questions. Rightfully so, this body of research is not intended to be a capstone; rather it is to be a catalyst to fulfilling my innate moral dedication to the work being done in public schools; specifically schools serving high numbers of children living in poverty.

It is my aim to employ Socio-Cultural Leadership behaviors as a practitioner. More importantly, it is my humble desire that school leaders all over the world make use of Socio-Cultural Leadership as a new starting point for the study of school leadership. In order for these aspirations to reach fruition, empirical inquiry into the limitations of this study's findings, alluded to earlier in this chapter, must be given persistent, mindful attention by anyone in a formal or informal capacity to persuade school leadership.

To people in positions of power who are responsible for hiring, evaluating, and retaining school principals, it is my request that each principal be a person who realizes the moral imperative of increasing student achievement for all students. In addition, each principal should be able to combine intellectual capacity, social awareness, managerial astuteness, and political acumen, in the absence of research-proven leadership strategies, to meet the social and academic needs of all students; paying special attention to children living in poverty.

About the Author

Desmond K. Blackburn, of Weston, Florida, began his professional educational career in 1996. Since then, Dr. Blackburn has served one of the largest urban school districts in the United States as a high school math teacher, a middle school assistant principal, a middle school principal, a district trainer, and a director of school improvement. He is an educational leadership adjunct professor at a local university. He is also the CEO and President of D & G Leadership, Inc., a full-service educational consulting firm.

Dr. Blackburn earned a Bachelor of Science in Mathematics from the University of Florida; a Master of Science in Educational Leadership from Nova Southeastern University; and a Doctorate of Philosophy in Educational Leadership from Florida Atlantic University. He and his wife, Kelli, have two sons, Dean and Grant.

For more information on Desmond K. Blackburn or how D & G Leadership, Inc. can help your school, school district, college, or university meet its educational goals, visit www.dgleadership.com.

References

Ashkanasy, Neal M., & Dasborough, Marie T. (2003). Emotional awareness and emotional intelligence in leadership teaching. *Journal of Education for Business, 79*(1), 18-22.

Baker, Eva L., Betebenner, Damian W., & Linn, Robert L. (2002). Accountability Systems: Implications of Requirements of the No Child Left Behind Act of 2001. *Educational Researcher*, 31 (6), 3-16.

Barnett, Kerry, & McCormick, John (2004). Leadership and individual principal-teacher relationships in schools. *Educational Administration Quarterly, 40*(3), 406-434.

Bass, Bernard M., & Avolio, Bruce J. (1994). *Improving organizational effectiveness through transformational leadership.* Thousand Oaks, CA: Sage.

Bloom, Leslie R. (2003). I'm poor, I'm single, I'm a mom, and I deserve respect: Advocating in schools as mothers in poverty. *Educational Studies,* 300-316.

Bogotch, Ira E. (2002). Educational leadership and social justice: Practice into theory. *Journal of School Leadership, 12,* 138-155.

Bogotch, Ira E., Williams, Paul, Jr., & Hale, Jim (1995). School managerial control: Validating a social concept. *Journal of Educational Administration, 33*(1), 44-62.

Bolman, Lee G., & Deal, Terrence E. (1997). *Reframing organizations.* San Francisco: Jossey-Bass.

Bowman, Richard F. (2004). Teachers as leaders. *The Clearing House, 77*(5), 187-189.

Brown, Kathleen M., & Anfara, Vincent A., Jr. (2003). Paving the way for change: Visionary leadership in action at the middle level. *NASSP Bulletin, 87*(635), 16-34.

Bulman, Robert C. (2002). Teachers in the 'hood: Hollywood's middle-class fantasy. *The Urban Review, 34*(3), 251-276.

Checkley, Kathy (2004). A is for audacity: Lessons in leadership from Lorraine Monroe. *Educational Leadership, 61*(7), 70-72.

Chirichello, Michael (2004). Collective leadership: Reinventing the principalship. *Kappa Delta Pi, 40*(3), 119-123.

Clark, Don, Petzko, Vicki, & Valentine, Jerry (2004, November 5). *A national study of highly successful principals and how they influence school programs and practices.* Paper presented at National Middle School Association Annual Conference.

Cobb, Charlene (2004). Effective instruction begins with purposeful assessments. *Read Teach, 57*(4), 386-388.

Collins, Janet (2000). Are you talking to me? The need to respect and develop a pupil's self-image. *Educational Research, 42*(2), 157-166.

Cunningham, Chris. (2004). Engaging the community to support student success. *Teacher Librarian, 31*(4), 33-36.

Decker, Larry E., & Decker, Virginia A. (2003). *Home, school, and community partnerships.* Oxford, UK: The Scarecrow Press.

Dewey, John (1909). *Moral principles in education.* Southern Illinois University: Center of Dewey Studies.

Doyle, Lynn H. (2004). Leadership for community building: Changing how we think and act. *Clearing House, 77*(5), 196-199.

DuFour, Richard (2002). The learning-centered principal. *Educational Leadership, 59*(8), 12-15.

DuFour, Richard P. (1991). *The principal as staff developer.* Bloomington, IN: National Education Service.

Dulewicz, Victor, & Higgs, Malcolm (1998). Emotional intelligence: Can it be measured reliably and validly using competency data? *Competency, 6*(1).

Feist, Gregory J., & Barron, F. (1996, June). *Emotional intelligence and academic intelligence in career and life success.* Paper presented at the Annual Convention of the American Psychological Society.

Fiore, Douglas (2000). Positive school cultures: The importance of visible leaders. *Contemporary Education, 71*(2), 11-13.

Foster, William (1986). *Paradigms and promises.* Amherst, NY: Prometheus Books.

Foster, William P. (2004). The decline of the local: A challenge to educational leadership. *Educational Administration Quarterly, 40*(2), 176-191.

Fullan, Michael (2001). *Leading in a culture of change.* San Francisco: Jossey-Bass.

Fullan, Michael (2003). *The moral imperative of school leadership.* Thousand Oaks, CA: Corwin Press, Inc.

Fullan, Michael, & Hargreaves, Andy (1996). *What's worth fighting for in your school.* New York: Teachers College Press.

Giesen, Judy, & Newton, Rose M. (2004, April 13). *The research challenge: Identifying the relative importance of attributes of the principalship.* Paper presented at the Annual Meeting of the American Educational Research Association.

Ginwright, Shawn A. (2000). Identity for sale: The limits of racial reform in urban schools. *The Urban Review, 32*(1), 87-104.

Glickman, Carl (1985). *Supervision of instruction: A developmental approach.* Boston: Allyn & Bacon.

Goleman, Daniel (2002). *Primal leadership.* Boston: Harvard Business School Press.

Greenfield, William D., Jr. (2004). Moral leadership in schools. *Journal of Educational Administration, 42*(2), 174-196.

Gruenert, Steve W. (1998). Development of a school culture survey. *UMI Microform.* ProQuest Information and Learning Company, Ann Arbor, MI. (UMI No. 9901237)

Hallinger, Philip, & Murphy, Joseph (1985). Assessing the instructional management behavior of principals. *The Elementary School Journal, 86*(2), 217-247.

Harris, Alma (2000). What works in school improvement? Lessons from the field and future directions. *Educational Research, 42*(1), 1-11.

Heaney, Liam F. (2001). A question of management: Conflict, pressure, and time. *The International Journal of Educational Management, 15*(4), 197-203.

Hofstede, Geert (1997). *Cultures and organizations: Software of the mind.* New York: McGraw-Hill.

Holme, Jennifer J. (2002). Buying Homes, Buying Schools: Schools Choice and the Social Construction of School Quality. *Harvard Educational Review*, 72, 177-205.

Huber, Stephan G. (2004). School leadership and leadership development. *Journal of Educational Administration, 42*(6), 669-684.

Huffman, Jane (2003). The role of shared values and vision in creating professional learning communities [Special issue]. *National Association of Secondary Schools Principals, 87*(637), 21-34.

Iceland, John (2003). Why poverty remains high: The role of income growth, economic inequality, and changes in family structure, 1949-1999. *Demography, 40*(3), 499-519.

Interstate School Leaders Licensure Consortium. (1996, November 2). *Standards for school leaders*. Retrieved March 19, 2005, from http://www.nassp.org

Johnson, Mary (2003). *American schooling has failed children of color* [Essay].

Johnson, Ruth S. (2002). *Using data to close the achievement gap*. Thousand Oaks, CA: Corwin Press, Inc.

Kitano, Margie K. (2003). Gifted potential and poverty: A call for extraordinary action. *Journal for the Education of the Gifted, 26*(4), 292-303.

Kotter, John P. (1996). *Leading change*. Boston: Harvard Business School Press.

Lam, Shui-fong F., Yim, Pui-shan S., & Lam, Tom W. (2002). Transforming school culture: Can true collaboration be initiated? *Educational Research, 44*(2), 181-195.

Leithwood, Kenneth, & Jantzi, Doris (1999). The relative effects of principal and teachers sources of leadership on student engagement with school. *Educational Administration Quarterly, 35,* 679-706.

Leithwood, Kenneth, Steinbach, Rosanne, & Jantzi, Doris (2002). School leadership and teachers' motivation to implement accountability policies. *Educational Administration Quarterly, 38*(1), 94-119.

Lester, Paula E., & Bishop, Lloyd K. (2000). *Handbook of tests and measurement in education and the social sciences* (2nd ed.). London: Scarecrow Press.

Lezotte, Lawrence W. (1997). *Learning for all.* Okemas, MI: Effective Schools Product.

Ludwig, Jens (1999). Information and inner city educational attainment. *Economics of Education Review, 18,* 17-30.

Maxwell, John C. (2004). *Today matters.* Boston: Warner Faith.

McEwan, Elaine K. (1998). *Seven steps to effective instructional leadership.* Thousand Oaks, CA: Corwin Press, Inc.

Meece, Judith L. (2003). Applying Learner-Centered Principles to Middle School Education. *Theory Into Practice, 42*(2), 109-116.

Murphy, Joseph (2002). Reculturing the profession of educational leadership: New blueprints. *Educational Administration Quarterly, 38*(2), 176-191.

National Association of Elementary School Principals. (2001). NAESP redefines role of school principal.

National Association of Secondary School Principals. (2001). 21st century school administrator skills.

National Institute on Educational Governance, Finance, Policymaking, and Management. (1999). *Effective leaders for today's schools.* Washington, DC: U.S. Department of Education Office of Educational Research and Improvement.

Noguera, Pedro A. (2003). Schools, prisons, and social implications of punishment: Rethinking disciplinary practices. *Theory into Practice, 42*(4), 341-350.

Northouse, Peter G. (2001). *Leadership: Theory and practice* (2nd ed.). Thousand Oaks, CA: Sage Publications.

Pajak, Edward (1993). *Approaches to clinical supervision: Alternatives for improving instruction.* Norwood, MA: Christopher-Gordon.

Payne, Ruby K. (1998). *A framework for understanding poverty.* Baytown, TX: RFT Publishing.

Peacock, M. Jean, McClure, Faith, & Agars, Mark D. (2003). Predictors of delinquent behaviors among Latino youth. *The Urban Review, 35*(1), 59-72.

Robbins, Harvey, & Finley, Michael (1997). *Why change doesn't work.* Princeton, NJ: Peterson's.

Rogers, Judy L. (1988). New paradigm leadership. *Initiatives, 51*(4), 1-8.

Rosenblatt, Zehava (2004). Skill flexibility and school change: A multi-national study. *Journal of Educational Change, 5,* 1-30.

Sanders, Mavis, & Harvey, Adia (2002). Beyond the school walls: A case study of principal leadership for school-community collaboration. *Teachers College Record, 104*(7). Retrieved May 1, 2004, from http://www.tcrecord.org

Schein, Edgar (1992). *Organizational culture and leadership.* San Francisco: Jossey-Bass.

Schlechty, Philip C. (2002). *Working on the work: An action plan for teachers, principals, and superintendents.* San Francisco: Jossey-Bass.

Schon, Don (1988). Reflection in teacher education. In *Coaching reflecting teaching* (pp. 19-30). New York: Teachers College Press.

Senge, Peter M. (1990). *The fifth discipline.* New York: Doubleday.

Sergiovanni, Thomas J. (1992). *Moral leadership: Getting to the heart of school improvement.* San Francisco: Jossey-Bass.

Shields, Carolyn M. (2004). Dialogic leadership for social justice: Overcoming pathologies of silence. *Educational Administration Quarterly, 40*(1), 109-132.

Shukla-Mehta, Smita, & Albin, Richard W. (2003). Twelve practical strategies to prevent behavioral escalation in classroom settings. *The Clearing House, 77*(2), 50-56.

Smith, Nancy J. (2004, April 15). *Democratic leadership and moral leadership: exploring the connection from a pragmatic perspective.* Paper presented at the American Educational Research Association Annual Meeting.

Spencer, Lyle, & Spencer, Signe (1993). *Competence at work.* New York: John Wiley.

Sullivan, Susan, & Glanz, Jeffrey (2000). *Supervision that improves teaching: Strategies and techniques.* Thousand Oaks, CA: Corwin Press.

Tyack, David B. (1974). *The one best system.* Boston: Harvard University Press.

Villa, Celestine (2003). Community building to serve all students. *Education, 123*(4), 777-779, 814.

Weinstein, Carol, Curran, Mary, & Tomlinson-Clarke, Saundra (2003). Culturally responsive classroom management: Awareness into action. *Theory into Practice, 42*(4), 269-276. Whitaker, Beth (1997). Instructional leadership and principal visibility. *The Clearing House, 70*(Fall), 155-156.

Whitaker, Todd, Whitaker, Beth, & Lumpa, Dale (2000). *Motivating & inspiring teachers.* Larchmont, NY: Eye on Education, Inc.

Witzers, Bob, Bosker, Roel J., & Kruger, Meta L. (2003). Educational leadership and student achievement: The elusive search for an association. *Educational Administration Quarterly, 39*(3), 398-425.

Yep, Maureen, & Chrispeels, Janet H. (2004, April 14). *Principals reflect on sharing leadership.* Paper presented at the Annual Meeting of the American Educational Research Association.

Zepeda, Sally J. (2004). Leadership to build learning communities. *The Educational Forum, 68*(2), 144-151.

www.ingramcontent.com/pod-product-compliance
Lightning Source LLC
Chambersburg PA
CBHW020340290526
45785CB00005B/2112